W9-CMG-048

SEX IS A PARENT AFFAIR

BY LETHA SCANZONI

G/L
REGAL
BOOKS
™

A Division of G/L Publications
Glendale, California, U.S.A.

Published by
Regal Books Division, G/L Publications
Glendale, California 91209, U.S.A.

Library of Congress Catalog Card No. 72-77114
Hard cover edition: ISBN 0-8307-0228-8
Soft cover edition: ISBN 0-8307-0160-5

Table of Contents

Abortion
Adoption
Adultery
Artificial Insemination
Birth Control
Circumcision
Crush
Exhibitionism
Fornication
Homosexuality
Marriage
Masturbation
Menopause
Menstruation
Multiple Births
Nudity
Petting
Pornography
Prostitution
Rape
Sex Slang
Sex Thoughts and Fantasies
Sexual Intercourse
Sterility and Sterilization
Venereal Diseases

Foreword

Sex education is a very frightening and bewildering subject to many Christian parents today. Their children are growing up in a highly eroticized society which bombards them with harmful sexual attitudes from every side. And although the biblical standards of morality have not changed, those traditional guidelines are being assaulted, contradicted and ridiculed throughout our culture.

This parental responsibility is much more difficult in an urban setting than it was "back on the farm." Children today are far removed from the animal life which was so helpful to Farmer John in teaching the facts of life to his inquisitive son. I discovered quite by accident, for example, that my city-born five-year-old thought "pigs give us ham" in much the same way "chickens give us eggs." Thus, lacking assistance from mother nature, sex education today often amounts to one massive, tension-filled adolescent conversation in the living room, leaving all participants in a state of utter exhaustion.

There must be a better way, and Mrs. Scanzoni has presented it in her book, SEX IS A PARENT AFFAIR. She approaches this sensitive matter of sex education with openness and candor, inspiring confidence in the reader. Her technical explanations are easily understood, even by the least informed parents, and she offers a useful introduction to the anatomy and physiology of sex. Of greater importance, however, are the healthy sexual attitudes which pervade her book. Mrs. Scanzoni has managed to underscore the biblical basis for morality and decency without making sex dirty and distasteful.

Mrs. Scanzoni's book is geared primarily for the parent who isn't too well acquainted with his own body and needs a concise review before teaching his children about theirs. Her recommendations are psychologically sound, and if applied, should lead our children to a proper view of sex as God intended. Overall, I believe Mrs. Scanzoni has written a timely book which will be of considerable help within the context of the Christian family.

James C. Dobson
USC School of Medicine

Preface

All of us are here because of sex. And we're parents because of sex. In the design of God, human life is passed on through the meeting of an ovum and sperm cell as a man and woman join their bodies in an act so intimate that the Bible says they become "one flesh."

As new little lives spring from this one-flesh relationship, parents continually realize what a great responsibility has been entrusted to them by God. They want to do their very best to help their children develop physically, socially, emotionally, intellectually, and spiritually.

Most parents know that an important part of this responsibility is providing their children with information and guidance in sexual matters. But often the task seems extremely difficult. Parents themselves are often unsure of many facts about sex, and they feel overwhelmed by the thought of teaching their children in this area. Some mothers and fathers feel timid, afraid, embarrassed, even ashamed when they think about the subject of sex— usually because wrong ideas were passed on to them during their own growing-up days. And to add to their fears and confusion, they constantly hear and read about ways traditional moral values are being questioned and even discarded by many today. Furthermore, young people are now exposed to areas of sexual knowledge that were never discussed publicly until very recently. How can parents dare to hope they'll be able to answer the kinds of questions that may come up in such an open setting?

Many Christian parents feel somewhat helpless. They

don't want to appear narrow and behind-the-times. But neither do they want to condone a permissiveness that flaunts the clear teaching of Scripture. They certainly don't want to ignore or stifle their youngsters' questions and break down communication in such a crucial area of life. But how can they deal with the specific matters young people are wondering about? How can they answer the questions of wide-eyed preschoolers who are curious about all the wonderful things awaiting discovery in the world around them—including sex? Or those of older children who need guidance in sorting out facts from the distorted half-truths and falsehoods they can't help but run up against in modern society? How can parents help teen-agers to develop wholesome attitudes toward human sexuality and a biblical view of sex ethics to guide them in sexual behavior?

Many parents are asking for help in the area of sex education in the Christian home. Down deep, they know that there must be ways to deal with questions that arise. They aren't despairing. There must be something they can do to help their children in their sexual understanding. "But how do we go about it?" they ask. "How can we prepare ourselves for the questions our children may ask? What kind of guidance can we give? How can we present the basic facts about sex? How can we answer some of the points older children might raise? How can we help young people gain both accurate information and the ability to view sex from a Christian perspective?"

It is for parents such as these—and with such questions in mind—that this book has been written.

Letha Scanzoni

Sex in God's Plan

Sex Was God's Idea

"When God created man, he made him in the likeness of God. Male and female he created them, and he blessed them and named them Man when they were created" (Genesis 5:1,2). It was *God* who designed human sexuality, and it was He who said in Genesis 1:31 that this was *very good*.

This is easy to forget in a society where not long ago sex was looked on as a thing of shame. Now it's almost worshiped as the goal of existence! But at either extreme, it's uncommon to think of sex in relation to God. "How in the world could sex have anything to do with God, or God with sex?" some people wonder. If they do think of God and sex at all, they usually think only in negative terms, that God doesn't look favorably on sex. Many in fact think that this is what Christianity teaches!

Why should this be? Why should people think that God doesn't like sex when He thought it up in the first place? There are many reasons—some stretching far back into church history. Others have to do with mistaken ideas about the human body. Certain Christian leaders were influenced by pagan philosophies that taught

1

the body is corrupt and a hindrance to man's true being which is his spirit. It was forgotten that God created us as *both* body and spirit and He cares about the total person.

The Bible tells us that our bodies are designed by God. They become temples for the Holy Spirit when we place our faith in Christ (1 Corinthians 6:19). God Himself took on a human body when He came to earth in the person of Jesus Christ (1 Timothy 3:16; John 1:14; Hebrews 10:5). Some day our bodies will be raised from the dead, as was His (1 Corinthians 6:13,14). For all these reasons and more, Christians should never look upon the human body as an object of shame. Rather, we should present our bodies as living sacrifices to God (Romans 12:1), glorify God in our bodies (1 Corinthians 6:20), and hand over to Him every part of our bodies (including our sexuality) to be used as instruments of righteousness in His service (Romans 6:13).

A biblical view of the human body is an important part of grasping a biblical view of sex. Yet many Christians, who never even heard of the pagan philosophies that influenced the early church leaders, have similar difficulties. Often it's because they misinterpret Paul's teachings and warnings about the sins of the flesh. Many Christians believe when Paul said "flesh" he meant "body" and this proves that the body with its desires and appetites hinders living a holy life!

But in Galatians 5:19-21 Paul lists some of the sins of the flesh the Christian must avoid. Some like fornication and drunkenness do involve the body. But notice how many of them are clearly sins of the mind, heart, and will. Sins like envy, dissension, anger, selfishness and idolatry are mentioned. When the Bible speaks about the "flesh with its passions and desires" which must be put to death (Galatians 5:24), it doesn't mean we must kill sex or become an ascetic and deny all physical appetites.

2

The word "flesh" used this way doesn't refer to the human body at all, but rather to the sinful side of human nature that rebels against God and insists on having its own way (Romans 8:7-9).

Early Christian leaders not only got off base in their attitudes toward the human body, but many developed wrong ideas about marriage. Some stressed that God was more pleased if people chose a life of celibacy. Marriage, they thought, was a hindrance to spiritual life. Part of such teachings arose from a downgrading of womanhood. Women were viewed as evil temptresses eager to seduce men and lead them away from God. Such ideas are not biblical. God instituted marriage, and it was at a wedding that Jesus performed His first miracle. Jesus often used marriage as an illustration of spiritual truth.

Even so, there were many Christian leaders who tried to show God disapproved of marriage for those who wished to be truly spiritual. They tried to support their views from Scripture, using Revelation 14:4 which speaks of 144,000 redeemed men who follow the Lamb of God. The verse says of them, "It is these who have not defiled themselves with women, for they are chaste." But in truth, the verse doesn't say sexual intercourse defiles a man. Rather, it points out these particular men obeyed God's standards of refraining from sexual relations apart from marriage. They had not committed fornication. However, some Christians used the passage otherwise and sought to downgrade womanhood, marriage, and sex.

It's amazing to read where some of these mistaken ideas led. There were some Christians who couldn't believe God designed human sexuality. They even suggested that the devil must have designed our sex organs!

Some early Christian leaders told married couples they weren't allowed to partake of the Lord's Supper for several days after having sexual intercourse. Some religious

3

officials even went to the trouble of making out a list of acceptable times when a husband and wife could copulate. It might be more accurate to call it a list of times when they should *not* have sex! They were supposed to refrain on Thursdays because Christ had been arrested on a Thursday, on Fridays because the Crucifixion took place on Friday, on Saturdays because the Virgin Mary was to be honored through sexual abstinence, on Sundays because Christ arose on the first day of the week, and on Mondays because this was a way to honor the dead. In other words, only two days a week were acceptable for sex! During the Middle Ages, there were theologians who told husbands and wives that the Holy Spirit leaves the room while a couple engages in sexual intercourse.[1]

To cite further examples is unnecessary. We can see that down through the ages misconceptions have crept into the thinking of Christians. And today we have inherited many of the same false notions about sex. Frequently this is why we're uneasy about discussing the subject with our children, why we feel nervous, unsure, even a bit ashamed about this whole business. We *want* to believe that sex is good, sacred, and something planned by God. Yet we're not always sure. And when we see sexual abuse around us, we're sometimes tempted to think that maybe the early church leaders were on the right track when they warned us about the evils and dangers of sex. Christian parents continue to feel confused and ill at ease as they wonder about presenting sex as a wholesome gift of God.

If we are to be of any real help to our children we must root out false notions and wrong attitudes that we ourselves may have about sex. But getting rid of *wrong* ideas isn't enough. We must really search the Scriptures so that we can develop right biblical attitudes. Only then can we build upon a base that will fulfill our parental re-

4

sponsibilities in providing a proper sex education for our children.

Biblical Sex Standards

A concise summary of scriptural teachings on sex is found in Hebrews 13:4, "Let marriage be held in honor among all, and let the marriage bed be undefiled; for God will judge the immoral and adulterous." Notice it makes four main points.

First, marriage is an honorable institution—something God wants us to esteem highly. It's not a matter to be treated lightly or ridiculed. It's serious, sacred, and wonderful.

As God intended it, marriage is a relationship—a living, vital, dynamic relationship that serves as a picture of how God related to His church. (See the books of Hosea and Ephesians 5:25-32.) Marriage is a holy commitment of a man and a woman to each other. It is a covenant (Malachi 2:14). Jesus spoke of this in Matthew 19 where He reminded His hearers of what God said at the very beginning when He created man and woman and brought them together to be husband and wife. "Have you not read that he who made them from the beginning made them male and female, and said, 'For this reason a man shall leave his father and mother and be joined to his wife, and the two shall become one'? So they are no longer two but one" (Matthew 19:4-6). In marriage a new social unit comes into being. The old family with one's parents is left and a new family with one's spouse is formed. Two have publicly declared their intention to share their lives together and have become "one flesh." God created man and woman to fit together, to be joined. Ideally, in sexual intercourse a couple is acting out the oneness that is already theirs in all other realms of the marital relationship.

Which brings out the second point made in Hebrews

5

13:4—that the marriage bed is something very special. It provides a unique means of refreshment and delight. A place of comfort, strengthening, invigoration, communion, and nurture. A place to which a husband and wife return again and again to experience the wonder of merging themselves with one another, the joy of being fused together, the thrill of physically expressing the deepest emotions of their hearts. God intended sex to be that way. And so the marriage bed must be kept undefiled. It must be guarded from anything that would detract from or spoil a couple's love and unity. Obviously, this means that there must be no room for unfaithfulness. Sex is to be reserved for a husband and wife alone. Their bodies belong only to each other and to God.

Not only is unfaithfulness forbidden but there must also be no exploitation—the use of sex as a weapon to dominate and manipulate in marriage. Anything that could hurt the spouse and bring disharmony into a marriage has no place in the relationship that God intended. In a sense, these things can defile or spoil the beauty of the marriage bed just as can unfaithfulness.

The third and fourth points made in Hebrews 13:4 have to do with God's judgment upon two forms of sexual sin. The first category mentioned is sometimes translated "the immoral" or "fornicators." The word, translated from the original Greek, means someone who is unmarried but who nevertheless finds a sexual partner and engages in copulation. This passage tells us that God is displeased with premarital sex. Christians are told to flee fornication (1 Corinthians 6:18; 1 Thessalonians 4:3).

But another category is also mentioned—the adulterous relationship. Married persons who have intercourse with somebody other than their spouse are guilty of the sin of *adultery*. Such persons have broken a commandment of God (Exodus 20:14); like those who commit fornication, they place themselves under God's judgment.

6

By no means is this to say that there is no forgiveness for sexual sins. Christ died for sinners, and we are *all* sinners. Sexual sins are no more beyond the scope of God's grace and Christ's shed blood than other sins. We'll discuss this and the implications of biblical teachings on fornication and adultery in a later chapter. We'll also be looking at what marriage and marital sex can and should be for the Christian. We will see how God's limits enhance rather than hamper our sexuality. But for the moment, let's consider Hebrews 13:4 to be a brief thumbnail sketch that will help us understand some of the most basic principles taught in Scripture. In sum, mainly this verse shows us that marriage is a good and honorable institution. Sex is an important part of marriage and should be recognized and treated accordingly. Fornication, or premarital sex, is displeasing to God and will be judged by Him. And adultery, or unfaithfulness to one's marriage partner and marriage vows, is likewise a sin in the sight of God.

Let's Talk It Over

Husbands and wives may find it profitable to talk over these questions and illustrations with one another. Also, parents meeting in classes and small groups may find they can stimulate one another's thinking by candidly discussing the material below, and bringing up new thoughts and questions.

1. In a women's Bible study, a Christian wife shared her feelings of distaste and shame whenever she and her husband had sexual intercourse following their devotional time. It seemed to take away the sacred, prayerful attitude, and made her feel almost unclean. Another woman present said her own experience was just the opposite. She and her husband felt closest to God and to each other after attending a service where they had partaken of the Lord's Supper. It was then that they felt most de-

7

sirous of the sexual embrace. Why do you think these women had such divergent viewpoints? How do you personally feel about their outlooks on sex and how it relates to God and one's spiritual life?

2. If adults have grown up with the idea that God frowns upon sexual pleasure and that sex is "dirty," how can their outlooks be changed? Or is it too late?

3. Name some ways that our society keeps alive the notion that sex is something shameful. How do the biblical principles discussed throughout this chapter help provide answers to such ideas?

4. Give examples of sexual idolatry in modern society. Why do some people have the idea that sex is the be-all-end-all of life? What do the Scriptures say with respect to this exaggerated emphasis on the importance of sex? Keeping in mind that sex is a good gift of the Creator, use Romans 1:24,25 to illustrate what is actually taking place when people put sex at the center of their lives. What are they forgetting? How and why does sex become an "idol"? Relate to the first commandment (Exodus 20:3).

5. Drawing upon the material from this chapter, your own ideas and experiences, and any additional Scripture references you can remember, make a list of reasons why a Christian should not be ashamed of his body and its functions and should treat the human body with respect. Why is such an understanding basic in forming a Christian philosophy of sex to share with our children?

References

1. For further discussion on attitudes toward sex in the history of the church, see my book, *Sex and the Single Eye* (Grand Rapids: Zondervan Publishing House, 1968), especially chapter 2.

CHAPTER TWO

Sex and the Christian Parent

It was Christmas Eve and the Jackson family gathered around the fireside to sing carols and read the story of Jesus' birth. Nine-year-old Jeff read from the first chapter of Matthew. Suddenly at the close of verse 25 he exclaimed, "That doesn't make sense! It says Joseph didn't *know* Mary until after Baby Jesus was born!"

Embarrassed, Mr. Jackson said, "Well, here the word *know* means something different."

"What?" asked Jeff. "It just means he wasn't married to Mary yet," said Mrs. Jackson nervously.

This confused Jeff and his eleven-year-old sister Jill who said, "But the verse before that one says Joseph took Mary as his wife."

"It doesn't make sense," continued Jeff, "people don't marry somebody they don't even *know*. How could *knowing* her after the baby was born make Mary and Joseph married?"

Flustered, Mrs. Jackson turned to her husband, hoping he would know how to handle the situation. But he felt as ill at ease as his wife. At this point, Jill said, "I know what. Let's look it up in the new Bible they gave us at Sunday School. It puts everything in the kind of words we use today. I bet it will explain it."

When Jill returned from her room with the open Bible, she had a strange look on her face and said hesitantly, "I think it means sexual relations." Her mother gasped. With a "please explain" look on her face Jill waited for her parents to comment.

But Mr. Jackson just cleared his throat and said, "This has been an interesting discussion, but I think we'd better move on to the main point of the story, that Jesus is Immanuel—God with us—and He came into the world to save us from our sins. That's what Matthew is really interested in telling us in this passage. So let's not get sidetracked. Maybe we can talk about this some other time when you're older and can understand better. But right now let's get on with Christmas."

The Jackson family lost an excellent opportunity for positive sex education. Worse yet, the parents conveyed the attitude that sex was something embarrassing, unmentionable, and shameful and had no place in a discussion at family devotions. The children knew their parents were always eager to discuss other questions they asked. But this time, both parents seemed embarrassed, almost annoyed. Jill wanted to ask more, even though her father said they'd talk about it another time. Somehow she felt certain they wouldn't. "One thing's for sure," she thought, "*I'm* not going to bring it up again! I feel funny when mom and dad act so mixed-up and upset. It almost makes *me* want to help *them*."

Later that night as Martha and Tom Jackson retired, they independently thought about the incident. Both wondered why they had been disturbed and thrown off guard by their children's innocent and normal curiosity. But because sex was such an uncomfortable subject between them, they failed to share their thoughts with each other.

Martha lay thinking about her own frustrated feelings that sex was a part of marriage to be endured—a duty that must be performed for one's husband. Secretly she was glad Tom didn't bother her too often about sexual intercourse. When he did, he seemed satisfied to get it over with quickly. Sometimes she avoided it completely by complaining of a headache, fatigue, or by insisting there were pressing household chores at the moment.

As she lay in the dark with Tom beside her, she wondered *why* she felt this way. Many of the women's magazines she read presented enlightened views about women and sex. Some cited studies and statistics to show that women could enjoy sex as much or more than men. But the question was always the same. "Why don't I feel that way?" Martha thought about possible reasons. She thought of the crude way she had learned about sex from a fourth-grade school chum. It seemed so long ago. But so vivid.

Martha and Shirley, a skinny girl with pigtails, had been playing on the school yard swings on a bright sunny fall day when suddenly Shirley said, "Know where babies come from?" Innocently, Martha replied, "Yes, the doctor brings them in his little black bag." That, after all, was what her parents had always told her. Shirley laughed. "No!" she shouted from her swing. "They come out of the mother, just like when she goes to the bathroom." Shirley then embellished her story with slang words and raw details.

Shocked, Martha knew it couldn't be true. Because what Shirley was saying sounded dirty and ugly. But she thought maybe it was really true! Maybe that's why everybody acted so strange and awkward when she asked certain questions. Like the time her parents kept her away from her pet dog, Ginger, and the next day she

11

found her surrounded by a bunch of puppies. When Martha asked if there was a special "dog doctor" who brought baby puppies in a little black bag, her parents laughed and said "no." But when she asked how the puppies got there, Martha's parents told her she was too little to understand and would find out when she was older. Maybe that was it! Maybe Ginger had gone to the bathroom and puppies came out instead! And maybe, thought little Martha, maybe that will happen to me! The thought frightened her.

But Shirley wasn't finished. "Know something else?" she said. "Want to know how the baby gets up in the mother so it has to come out again?" Martha was curious and couldn't imagine what new revelations might be forthcoming. Awkwardly, Shirley tried to describe sexual intercourse, and what she said left Martha confused and afraid.

Shirley not only told what she had heard about the sex act, but tried to describe what she had actually seen. "My parents do it sometimes," she said. "And they don't know but I can watch them through the keyhole in their bedroom door. I can't see too much; the bed isn't in the right place. But I see quite a bit. They take off their clothes and crawl all over each other and it looks like they're fighting. But I guess they're not really hurting each other. It's funny, but sort of scary, to watch. Have you ever watched to see if your parents do that, Martha?"

Martha, almost at the point of tears, was pale with shock. "My parents never would do such a thing!" she exclaimed as she started to run away. "Besides, I don't like you to talk about things like that."

"If they don't do that," shouted Shirley, "how did you and your brother get here? And know something else? Your mother is going to have another baby. I heard my mom tell Mrs. Smith at the store yesterday."

12

With tears streaming down her face, Martha ran into the house, desperately wanting to ask her mother if it was all true, but afraid to ask. Afraid her mother might say "yes." For the next several months Martha watched her mother's swelling abdomen, and in March the family greeted twin girls. Martha had experienced her first lessons in sex education. And she never forgot them.

Nor did she forget other childhood memories. Like the boy in school who kept a mirror at his desk and turned it at an angle (from seat-level) as the girls walked by so that he could look up their dresses. She was horrified at his behavior and told her mother. "Such boys are nasty, dirty and evil," said her mother. "Nice girls stay away from them." Martha wondered why this part of her body brought such reactions and why boys wanted to focus their mirrors like that. But her mother wouldn't explain. She just said, "It doesn't matter why. He's just bad."

Martha also recalled the time in her early teens when her mother called her aside for a "little talk." She told her that she should not let boys touch her body and went on to say that boys and men are interested in only one thing from women.

During that conversation, which raised more questions in Martha's young mind than it answered, Martha's mother revealed something about her own feelings toward sex in marriage. She had told Martha that "good" women never enjoyed sex. It was a service or duty a wife must provide for her husband, or else he'd run after other women. "Men have to find their pleasure somewhere," she declared. "It's that animal instinct in them. And sometimes they act like animals. But it's just one of the crosses you have to bear if you're a woman."

Martha thought back over her childhood introduction to sex and then related it to her own failure earlier that evening when she could have helped her own children. She wondered why she had not pursued better sex edu-

13

cation on her own. Why had she taken the word of her mother and her mother's women friends about the "awfulness" of sex? Surely there must have been at least a few books she could have read. But where? She would have been ashamed and embarrassed beyond description to ask at the library!

She and Tom had read a marriage manual just before their wedding date. Still, she knew her basic attitude toward sex was mixed up with fear, shame and aversion. As a Christian, it occurred to Martha that maybe God provided some guidance from the Scriptures. She determined to check a concordance in the morning.

While Martha lay reminiscing, Tom also thought about his own failure to answer his children's questions. He knew it was unreal to postpone sex education. "In fact," he thought, "those kids probably know more about sex than I think they do." Tom also remembered his own curiosity as a youngster, such as the time he saw a certain four-letter word scrawled on a bridge and asked his mother what it meant. Exploding in rage, Tom's mother washed out his mouth with soap for pronouncing the word.

He thought of his high school days and stories he heard from guys in the locker rooms. He remembered the hayride with his church's youth group, and how he got slapped when he tried slipping his hand under a girl's blouse after the kids grouped into couples and were necking in the moonlight.

He remembered how his best friend Ed was forced to marry a girl he had gotten pregnant. And how his father had called him in and had hemmed and hawed before saying, "Tom, you know what happened to Ed. I don't want you to find yourself in the same sort of difficulty, so I think it's time we had a little man-to-man talk." Tom grinned, as he remembered his father's stumbling words, and how nervous, flustered and embarrassed his dad was as he tried to spell out information that Tom had known

14

for years! "But then," thought Tom, "*my* performance as a sex educator tonight wasn't any better. I missed a great opportunity with Jeff and Jill."

Tom then began to think about his own marriage, and how little interest Martha had in sex. "I guess that's why when I approach her I feel like I'm imposing or bothering her," he thought. "Yet a man has his rights. It's all part of the marriage contract. But sometimes I wish she enjoyed sex more and would be a little more active and sexy. On the other hand she would probably frighten me if she were."

It was hard for Tom to forget all his mom and dad used to say about purity, loveliness, femininity, and true womanhood. His father told him before he got married not to expect too much in the sexual realm. "It's loose women who like sex," his father said. "Good women never do. And no matter how much men like loose women for fun and thrills, it's good women they want to marry and be mothers of their children."

"Well," thought Tom, "if not liking sex is the way you measure goodness, Martha is really good! I wish sometimes I could talk to her about how she really feels. But I know that would never work. She'd be too embarrassed. Isn't it strange that a man and woman can sleep together for thirteen years, have sex relations, produce two kids, and yet can't talk about their sex life without feeling embarrassed, awkward and ill at ease! It doesn't make sense. I wonder if our own confusion, hangups, and fear of our sexuality might have something to do with our failure to answer the children's questions? Perhaps that's why I hurry through sex with Martha instead of taking time to prepare her, the way the marriage manual says I should."

Tom yawned and as he drifted off to sleep, he decided to make a serious effort to talk with his children in the morning.

Tom and Martha are on the right track as evidenced by their willingness to help their children understand that sex in marriage is not tainted or shameful. And if they follow through they will find the Bible has a great deal to say about sex education.

"I never dreamed the Scriptures had so much to say about sex!" said one surprised young husband at a couples' retreat in which the following information was presented. Let's move on and see what he meant.

Four Aspects of Sex Presented in the Bible

There are many ways to look at sex. And Scripture doesn't ignore any of them. Basically, the purpose of sexual activity is fourfold—procreation, recreation, communication, and release. This doesn't mean, of course, that all four aspects must be covered in every single act of copulation. One or two might be emphasized more than others, and some aspects might never come onto the scene. The most obvious is procreation. Whether because of birth control or stage of wife's menstrual cycle, not *every* sex act will result in the beginning of a pregnancy.

Procreation

Sex is the vehicle God designed for babies to come into the world. It was the way He planned the human race to reproduce itself. This is the most obvious function of sex, but it is not the *only* function. For this reason the Christian couple practicing family planning and using contraceptives need not fear that they are going against the revealed will of God.

The reproductive aspect of sex is mentioned at the very outset of creation. Just as God had commanded the fish and birds to be fruitful and multiply (Genesis 1:22), so He commanded man and woman (Genesis 1:28) to the end that the earth should be filled. Sex for procreation is also seen in Deuteronomy 7:13,14, where God's

16

people were told that faithfulness to His covenant and obedience to His commandment would result in human, animal, and plant fertility.

"He will love you, bless you, and multiply you; he will also bless the fruit of your body and the fruit of your ground, your grain and your wine and your oil, the increase of your cattle and the young of your flock, in the land which he swore to your fathers to give you. You shall be blessed above all peoples; there shall not be male or female barren among you, or among your cattle" (Deuteronomy 7:13,14).

Likewise the Psalms are full of references to the procreational side of sex. Psalm 127:3 calls children a heritage of the Lord and "the fruit of the womb a reward." In Psalm 128, the man who fears the Lord is told, "Your wife will be like a fruitful vine within your house; your children will be like olive shoots around your table." Psalm 139 beautifully conveys the sense of wonder felt by the Bible writers as they contemplated God's design of the human body and His plan for the ongoingness of human life.

"You made all the delicate, inner parts of my body, and knit them together in my mother's womb. Thank you for making me so wonderfully complex! It is amazing to think about. Your workmanship is marvelous—and how well I know it. You were there while I was being formed in utter seclusion!" (Psalm 139:13-15, *TLB*).

And so it is throughout the Scriptures and throughout human history. Procreation is a very important purpose of sex. But it is by no means the only purpose. Let's move on to a second aspect.

Recreation

At first many Christians may be shocked to learn that sex is for fun and recreation. That the Scriptures actually encourage the enjoyment and sensual delights of sex.

"But isn't that the world's way?" you ask. "How can a Christian think of sex in such terms? Isn't sex supposed to be sacred, and serious? Why this talk about recreation? Sex isn't a game!"

Yes, for the Christian couple, sex can be regarded as sacred—if by this we mean set apart for God—desirous of pleasing and experiencing God's blessing in our sex life as well as in every area of life. Yes, sex is serious—if by this we mean it's not something to be taken lightly or treated as a big joke. But that doesn't mean sex was intended to be grim and dull, or as a duty instead of a delight. The Bible makes it very clear that God intended sex to be immensely pleasurable (*fun,* if you please) for both husbands and wives.

It will be helpful to note that the Bible writers often used poetic language to describe sexual organs, drives, energies, desires, and outlets. A favorite symbol for sex in Scripture is water—fountains, streams, cisterns, springs, and wells. In Proverbs 5 the human desire for sexual pleasure is clearly recognized. But the young man who is being addressed is told that he must find this pleasure only in marriage, only with his wife. That God is watching and is displeased when one's "springs" or sexual powers are scattered promiscuously outside the marital bond. He must not embrace the bosom of an adultress, says the writer, but rather the bosom of his own wife. It is expected that he will find great joy, delight, and refreshment (re-creation) in her embrace. He is told:

"Let your fountain be blessed, and rejoice in the wife of your youth, a lovely hind, a graceful doe.

"Let her affection fill you at all times with delight, be infatuated always with her love" (Proverbs 5:18,19).

The word *affection* may also be translated *breasts.* Either is correct, and no doubt both ideas, emotional affection and the physical bosom, are intended. The word *in-*

fatuated is also interesting. It literally carries the idea of intoxication or being "led astray." The *Amplified Bible* captures the thought in the expression: "Always be transported with delight in her love." The thought is expanded even further in the *New English Bible:* "You will at all times be bathed in her love, and her love will continually wrap you round."

Being transported, bathed and wrapped around, by the spouse's love, the ecstasy experienced in the marital embrace is nothing short of sex being for pleasure and recreation. This means the enjoyment of sex is not to be denied. Why is the woman spoken of as a "lovely hind, a graceful doe"? The hind is the female red deer to which reference is made in Psalm 42, where the hart (the male deer) longs for flowing streams. The hind was known for its gracefulness and fleetness of foot, leaping and running gracefully over the fields and hills. The picture again suggests beauty, movement, playfulness, and sheer delight. Proverbs 5 makes no attempt to hide, deny, or gloss over the fact that the husband and wife come to their bed to experience sexual *pleasure*. Such a purpose of the marital embrace is not only mentioned without embarrassment, it is positively encouraged.

Communication

In the marriage relationship, sexual intercourse was also designed by God to provide a means of expressing the deep unity a husband and wife feel toward one another. There can also be a communion of spirits when there is a union of bodies. This may very well be why the Bible writers frequently used the word "know" when referring to sexual intercourse. See, for example, Genesis 4:1, where we're told that "Adam knew Eve his wife, and she conceived."

Ideally, sex provides a means in which a couple concretely illustrate the blending of spirits and intertwining of their souls. The intimacy known in being joined together physically can and should reflect shared intimacy in all other areas of life. They have become "one flesh" (Genesis 2:24) and are no longer two but one. Fused together, they find that sexual intercourse provides a beautiful picture of oneness.

In the plan of God, sex was intended to provide a means of totally revealing oneself to the beloved, of pouring one's energies and deepest affection, hopes, and dreams into the loved one. Sex provides a means of presenting one's spouse with the gift of oneself and experiencing a like gift in return; a means of saying, "I love you." In short, sex becomes a mode of communication, a means of "knowing" one another.

At this point, however, we must not be carried away and overlook the realities of married life. During the duration of a marriage—the total hours, days, months, and years a couple are together—only a tiny percentage of actual *time* is spent in sexual intercourse. Therefore, a couple must get to know one another in ways other than sexually. Communication in *all* areas of life is crucial in marriage. There is nothing magical about sex; intercourse does not have mystical powers that automatically transform a poor relationship into a good one. In fact, things seem to work the other way around. The more a husband and wife are open, honest, sharing, and communicative on other levels, the more likely it is that they will be able to approach sex as a further means of opening themselves up to one another.

Release

The fourth aspect of sex mentioned in the Bible has to do with sheer bodily release. The physical nature of sexual drives, tensions, and energies is very real, and the Scriptures recognize this. This is not to suggest that a life of celibacy is impossible, nor that sex must be seen as *the* all powerful force which drives our lives so that we're overwhelmed with passion and are helpless in resisting desire. The Bible has a great deal to say about self-control and God's enablement and strengthening in times of temptation.

Nevertheless, there are cases in which circumstances combine to produce sexual tensions at a very high level. And it was such a situation which confronted the Christians of long ago Corinth when Paul wrote to them. Many had been converted out of a paganism which highly exalted sex and included sexual practices in its worship. Hundreds of prostitute-priestesses were employed in Corinth's temple dedicated to the goddess Aphrodite. Corinth had the reputation of being a swinging city, and sexual excesses of every sort were practiced.

Many of the Corinthian Christians were converted to Christ after having lived lives where fornication, adultery, and homosexual acts were not uncommon (see 1 Corinthians 6:9-11). Thus, in the midst of such surroundings, it isn't surprising that even after conversion they continued to have problems in their sex lives.

It was for this reason that Paul encouraged marriage, maintaining this was the way God provided as an outlet for sexual release. This would prevent fornication (1 Corinthians 7:2). At the same time, Paul knew married couples might be tempted to seek sexual release elsewhere if they abstained from marital relations for too long a time, (1 Corinthians 7:5). The apostle expressed a wish that all might have the gift of continence as he did, but he knew this was unrealistic. He was aware of the buildup of sexual tensions and the longing for sexual release. "If they cannot exercise self-control," wrote Paul, "they should marry. For it is better to marry than to be aflame with passion" (1 Corinthians 7:9). A similar thought occurs in verse 36.

Unfortunately, many Christians over the ages have

21

acted as though this is the Bible's sole teaching on marriage and theologians have thus spoken of marriage as a remedy, a medicine, to alleviate the problem of lust. By thinking in such terms, they've forgotten the communicative companionship side of marriage and the enrichment that sex brings to a couple. By viewing marriage as a way of *curing* sexual tensions—and viewing the wife as a "thing" to be used, some Christians forgot that the wife was a partner with whom to share a life. This is not the fault of the apostle Paul. His advice was wise and suited to the situation about which the Corinthian Christians had written him. Unfortunately various church leaders misinterpreted and misapplied some of Paul's teachings and presented a distorted view of the marriage relationship as God planned it in the beginning.

That God planned for sex to act as a physical release is as clear and real as the other three aspects of sex. This is particularly true in situations in which persons are constantly confronted by sexual stimuli, as was true in ancient Corinth and may be increasingly true in our own society. Implications of this will be discussed in later chapters.

The Biblical Ideal
of Sex in Marriage—Joyous Sexuality

Having seen then that sex is for procreation, recreation, communication, and release, let's briefly consider what an awareness of this fourfold purpose might mean for a married couple. First of all, it could bring a new sense of discovery and a refreshing new outlook to their sex life. It could help husbands and wives to "let themselves go." It could put away inhibitions and free feelings they may have held in check believing these desires and impulses to be evil and unspiritual. It could remove the sense of guilt that Christian couples sometimes feel when they find themselves actually *enjoying* sex.

22

In saying that "joyous sexuality" is the biblical ideal, I'm suggesting that a great deal of emphasis in the Scriptures seems to point toward a combination of the communication-recreation aspects of sex. Procreation and release fit easily into this and may be byproducts. But communication and recreation touch upon the inner feelings and attitudes of the husband and wife. These aspects of sex call for total involvement on an emotional-mental-spiritual level as well as on the physical. Joyous sexuality means vividly experiencing a sense of oneness with one another in an atmosphere of great delight.

This means there must be a reciprocal giving of each other. Sex was never intended by God to be one-sided. It should be desired and enjoyed by both husband and wife. In a marriage where this is not true, the couple should openly discuss and seek a joint solution to their problem. The Bible makes it clear that both men and women have sexual desires.

In the past, our culture has suppressed the fact that women have sexual desires, giving rise to the myth that women don't care much about sex. But recent research makes it clear that where women have been little interested in sex it has been due to the way society has molded women, the way women have been taught to think and feel. Disinterest in sex is *not* part of female nature, not something women are born with, not something natural.

Scientific research, especially that of Masters and Johnson in their book, *Human Sexual Response,* and other writings, has shown that the sexual capacities and desires of women equal and often exceed those of men. Women have been shown, for example, to have the capacity for very great response to stimulation of the clitoris (the small, sensitive external sex organ in front of the vaginal opening), and it is not unusual for women to experience multiple orgasms during intercourse. Women are *not* by nature reticent, reluctant, passive, and sexually indifferent (although they may be so by learning). There is no reason why a wife shouldn't bring just as much vitality, creativity, energy, and enjoyment to the marital embrace as does her husband.

This spontaneity shouldn't be threatening to the husband. In fact, it can make sex really great for him! He receives as well as gives; he is loved as well as loving. For too long, men have been encouraged to think of sex in terms of conquest and dominance. The image has been one of "conquering," "mastering," and "penetrating," an act by a male performed on a female—something "done to" a woman. Rather, the image should be one of interconnection, mutual sharing, union and oneness.

Some writings have even suggested that men *by their very nature* cannot help but think of sex in terms of "proving their masculinity," demonstrating their power over women, with each sex act viewed as a sheer act of courage. It is unfortunate that Christians have sometimes adopted such thinking, because it isn't verified by the Scriptures. Look, for example, at 1 Corinthians 7:3,4: "The husband should give to his wife her conjugal rights, and likewise the wife to her husband. For the wife does not rule over her own body, but the husband does; likewise the husband does not rule over his own body, but the wife does."

The passage makes it clear that both marital partners have sexual needs and desires. The husband "owes" it to his wife to bring her sexual pleasure, just as she "owes" it to her husband. There is no hint whatsoever that this is something one-sided. Both men and women are sexual beings. Both are to be active sexually within the relationship of marriage.

There are at least two implications of this. First, it means that since a wife has the same sexual desires as her husband, and his body belongs to her just as her body belongs to him, there is no reason why she shouldn't initiate sex relations when she desires. She needn't wait for him to ask her because she fears that to approach him would mean she is acting unfeminine, bold and aggressive. If a wife loves her husband and wants to show that love physically, she isn't being aggressive, but rather expressive. This doesn't mean that a wife demands that her husband drop everything and have sex with her immediately, displaying an attitude of, "Look, your body belongs to me and I have my rights and I want you right now." And the same is true for the husband in his approach to his wife.

In both cases, tenderness, love, and playfulness are in order, but *not* an attitude of domineering or an emphasis on duty or any hint of selfishly desiring to use one another. Either husband or wife can approach the other with an attitude of, "Darling, you're really the greatest. You really turn me on! I love you so much it seems I can never get enough of you, never get close enough to you. You mean so very much to me. Let's have a time of loving. I want to show you what I'm feeling toward you."

A second implication of the emphasis on the equality stressed in 1 Corinthians 7:3,4 has to do with the active participation of both husband and wife during the entirety of the sex act. There should be no inhibitions, no hesitations in caressing and enjoying each other's bodies. God created our bodies in such a way that they would be able to experience such pleasure. It is not evil or dirty or sinful. It is good.

The marriage bed is to be honored and received with thanksgiving to the Creator who designed our bodies so that a husband and wife can know these special delights of love. Both husband and wife should give themselves freely and fully to the other and should likewise receive the other in grateful delight. Each should be sensitive to the other's needs, likes, and dislikes with regard to sex and should do everything possible to raise the partner's thrill and ecstasy to the highest possible level. The murmurs, sighs and squeals of enjoyment and contentment can show the spouse what is most pleasurable, as can simple verbal expressions like, "That feels so good," or "Do that some more, Honey; I like it."

An increasing number of Christian theologians and writers have suggested that God gave the Song of Solomon to show us what joyous sexuality can be and to assure us that it is good. The Song of Solomon is a love poem and shows the joy of two newlyweds as they delight fully in one another and experience the wonder of the sexual expression of that love.

Often this book of the Bible is read for its devotional teachings portraying the love of Christ, the divine Bridegroom, for His Bride, the Church. And such an application is certainly in keeping with such passages as Ephesians 5:25-32 and Revelation 19:7-9. However, this doesn't blot out the fact that the book is basically a song of marital love, including the physical expression of the one-flesh relationship. In fact, one might argue that if God didn't reveal to us the ideal of marital love as He intended it to be, how could we be expected to understand the analogy in which Christ and His Church are compared to husband and wife?

Husbands and wives would find it profitable to read the Song of Solomon aloud together in a contemporary translation of the Bible. Parts may seem hard to understand, especially since it is written as poetry, with the bride speaking sometimes, the bridegroom at other times, and a chorus reciting at still other times. In addition, there are "flashbacks," reminiscences of earlier scenes, feelings, and happenings. Yet, the main idea of the book comes through very clearly: This is a husband and wife who mutually and utterly delight in one another.

The bride says of her husband, "My beloved is to me a

bag of myrrh that, lies between my breasts" (1:13); and he says of her, "Behold, you are beautiful, my love; behold you are beautiful; your eyes are doves. . . . O my dove, in the clefts of the rock, in the covert of the cliff, let me see your face, let me hear your voice, for your voice is sweet, and your face is comely" (1:15; 2:14). He tells her that compared to other girls she's like a lily among brambles (2:2), and she tells him that compared to other young men he's like a fruit-laden apple tree standing out among trees of ordinary wood. She is very conscious of physical desire and feels lovesick (2:5), and longs for his embrace (2:6).

But it isn't only physical desire they feel toward one another. Their love goes far deeper. They relate as persons, not only as bodies. The wife says her husband is altogether desirable (5:16). He is not only her beloved but is also her friend (5:16). To know they belong to one another totally fills her with great joy. "My beloved is mine and I am his" (2:16).

The bridegroom tells his wife that she has ravished his heart (4:9).

"How sweet is your love, my sister, my bride! how much better is your love than wine, and the fragrance of your oils than any spice! Your lips distil nectar, my bride; honey and milk are under your tongue; the scent of your garments is like the scent of Lebanon. A garden locked is my sister, my bride, a garden locked, a fountain sealed" (Song of Solomon 4:10-12).

The imagery of fountains and gardens is again used, reminding us of the description of sex that we saw in Proverbs 5. Here on their wedding night, the bride is described as a locked garden (a symbol of virginity)—a garden filled with beauty, fragrance, luscious fruits, and flowing streams. The wife invites her husband to enter the garden, which she now calls *his* garden for she is presenting herself to him as he is presenting himself to her.

"Awake, O north wind, and come, O south wind! Blow upon my garden, let its fragrance be wafted abroad. Let my beloved come to his garden, and eat its choicest fruits" (4:16).

And her husband responds:

"I come to my garden, my sister, my bride, I gather my myrrh with my spice, I eat my honeycomb with my honey, I drink my wine with my milk."

Both husband and wife experience ecstatic rapture, and the chorus sings:

"Eat, O friends, and drink: Drink deeply, O lovers!" (5:1).

Throughout the book, we see that both husband and wife actively participate in the physical expression of their love and unity. Neither feels any sense of shame or inhibition in the adoration of one another's bodies. Notice some of the ways the bride describes her beloved:

"My beloved is all radiant and ruddy, distinguished among ten thousand. . . . His cheeks are like beds of spices, yielding fragrance. His lips are lilies, distilling liquid myrrh. His arms are rounded gold, set with jewels. His body is ivory work, encrusted with sapphires. His legs are alabaster columns, set upon bases of gold. His appearance is like Lebanon, choice as the cedars" (5:10,13-15).

Similarly the bride is beautiful in her husband's eyes, and he describes her in such words as these:

"Your rounded thighs are like jewels, the work of a master hand. . . . Your two breasts are like two fawns, twins of a gazelle. Your neck is like an ivory tower" (7:1,3,4).

And what deep desire her loveliness arouses in him!

"How fair and pleasant you are, O loved one, delectable maiden! You are stately as a palm tree, and your breasts are like its clusters. I say I will climb the palm tree and lay hold of its branches. Oh, may your breasts

28

be like clusters of the vine, and the scent of your breath like apples, and your kisses like the best wine that goes down smoothly, gliding over lips and teeth" (7:6-9).

The bride is delighted and exclaims with joy and wonder, "I am my beloved's, and his desire is for me!" (7:10). She speaks of giving him her love and again reminds him that all the fruits of her love have been laid up for him alone (7:10-13).

This book suggests clearly that God intended the marital embrace to be an experience which brings great joy, thrill, and delight to both partners. God designed the human body to experience such sexual pleasure. And to think that such pleasure is wrong and evil is to insult the Creator who gave it to us as a good gift. It was God who made those special zones of the body which are so sexually sensitive. It was He who created the special nerve endings and impulses that result in such warm, pleasing and exciting feelings and sensations. It cannot be emphasized too strongly (because it has been so misunderstood and ignored in the past): Wives as well as husbands were given by God the capacity to find great delight in sexual intercourse. In this regard, a statement by sex researchers William Masters and Virginia Johnson is of interest:

"The clitoris is a unique organ in the total of human anatomy. Its express purpose is to serve both as a receptor and a transformer of sensual stimuli. Thus, the human female has an organ system which is totally limited in physiologic function to initiating or elevating levels of sexual tension. No such organ exists within the anatomic structure of the human male."[1]

In other words, God has provided women with an organ with no other purpose whatsoever but that of *sexual enjoyment*. It was not put there as a necessity for sexual intercourse, that is, it's possible for a woman's vagina to receive her husband's penis totally apart from the part played by the clitoris. Yet, the clitoris has been provided to make this an act of supreme enjoyment for both partners, making it possible for a woman to experience the explosive ecstasy of orgasm just as does her husband. (An interesting sidelight: Ancient love literature from eastern cultures refers to the clitoris as the "doorlatch" and the vagina as a temple to be entered. It is possible that the wife's thrill referred to in Song of Solomon 5:4 when her husband put his hand on the latch may be a reference to clitoral stimulation.)

Thus, sexual play—fondling of one another's sex organs—is not only acceptable but is important and desirable in sexual intercourse. Ample time should be allowed so that there can be much kissing, caressing, and petting included as *part* of the sex act. This should not just be considered as a prelude to the "real thing," but rather a total time of loving both before the actual merging of their bodies and afterwards as they bask in the glow of their love. Actually it might be better if intercourse were thought of not so much as the sex *act* but rather as the sex *relationship*—or even more accurately, as one expression of an overall, total relationship.

Notice that the poetic imagery in the Song of Solomon suggests a spirit of playfulness and frolicking merriment in the sexual embrace. Earlier we saw how Proverbs 5 referred to the wife as a lovely doe, a deer known for energy, fleetness, grace, and beauty. Here, too, similar imagery occurs. The bride speaks of her husband as a young stag "leaping upon the mountains, bounding over the hills" (Song of Solomon 2:8,9). She sees herself not only as a garden for her husband to enter and a palm tree he wishes to climb, but also views the soft round curves of her perfumed body as "hills of spices" which bring delight to her husband and result in pleasure to herself as well. She says:

"Make haste, my beloved, and be like a gazelle or a

young stag upon the mountains of spices" (Song of Solomon 8:14).

This then is the picture of joyous sexuality in married love that the Bible holds out to those who "have ears to hear." If we as parents can bring our own attitudes in line with this view, we have taken a major step in preparing ourselves to help our children form healthy, wholesome, biblical attitudes toward the gift of sex that God has given.

Let's Talk It Over

1. The following quotation is from a book for medical doctors. In what sense is it applicable to *parents* as well as to physicians?

"In our pursuit of continuing education in sexuality, it is not enough to limit education to outward means, but we must move toward an inward evaluation. It would be well for any physician dealing with young people today to have some long, frank discussions with wife, colleague, or friend about one's own triumphs, disappointments, and problems and one's personal moral views, since formulating these into words clears thoughts and often reveals embarrassing and previously unexpressible emotions that might otherwise surprise one during counseling. If we are unable to discuss our own sexuality, it will probably be unfair to discuss another's questions or problems, for we are too deeply involved in personal, unsolved emotional and moral problems."[2]

2. Have you ever encountered a problem similar to that of the Jackson family with regard to sex questions that came up during a family worship or in teaching Sunday School—that is, questions that were prompted by something in the Bible? (For example, a child may have

asked what a virgin is or what circumcision means.)
How did you handle it?

3. Why do you think husbands and wives often feel uncomfortable about discussing sex with one another? How can this problem be resolved?

4. Think back on your own childhood as Martha and Tom Jackson did.

    a. What was the first question about sex you can remember asking your parents? How did they respond?

    b. From what source (for example, parents, friends, books) did you first learn the basic facts about reproduction? Can you remember how you felt upon receiving this information?

    c. Most children are curious about their own sexual organs and those of their playmates. Were you ever made to feel ashamed of such curiosity? (For example, you may have been playing doctor and were scolded for conducting an innocently undertaken "physical exam.")

    d. Were you ever rebuked or punished after a parent or other adult caught you masturbating? How did you react? Did you feel that the body's pleasurable sensations must be evil?

    e. If you are a man, how did you learn about nocturnal emissions or "wet dreams"? How did you feel the first time you had such an experience?

    f. If you are a woman, how did you learn about menstruation? What were your thoughts and feelings when you had your first period?

5. Is the biblical view of marital sex as presented in this chapter new to you? Do you feel this outlook could be helpful in your own marriage? How could such an approach free Christian couples from feelings of guilt, fear, and shame in the marriage bed? How does the Song of Solomon suggest that the sexual expression of love is not

rigid and static but allows plenty of room for imaginativeness, creativity, and experimentation in position, practices, and techniques relating to sexual intercourse?

References

1. William Masters and Virginia Johnson, *Human Sexual Response* (Boston: Little, Brown and Company, 1966), as reprinted in Cecil E. Johnson, ed., *Sex and Human Relationships* (Columbus, Ohio: Charles E. Merrill Publishing Co., 1970), p. 131.

2. William A. Daniel, Jr., *The Adolescent Patient* (Saint Louis: The C. V. Mosby Company, 1970), p. 76.

CHAPTER THREE

Guidelines in Teaching
Your Children About Sex

"When it comes to discussing sex," said a teen-ager to his Sunday School teacher, "most adults are dishonest and evasive. I would like to talk to my parents about sex and some of the questions that bother me, but I can't. I don't feel free with my mom and dad."

It's no secret that many parents have great difficulty keeping lines of communication open between themselves and their children. And on no subject is this more true than the subject of sex. This isn't surprising. Thinking and talking about sex is powerful enough to stir up all sorts of emotions and reactions. It's hard to talk about sex as casually as we talk about the weather. The relationship between a man and a woman is deep and tremendously important. As parents, we're aware of that importance, and know a mistake in the area of male-female relationships can tragically affect a person's entire life.

On the other hand, we know that sex in marriage is a glorious, beautiful relationship that can enhance every

35

aspect of one's being. But how can a parent get this across to his child? Not sure of an answer to that question, many parents keep quiet.

Because of such hesitations, only a small percentage of young people receive their sex education from their parents. Surveys show children are more likely to learn about sex from their peers, and many times what they learn is incorrect.

Yet, it doesn't have to be that way. The second half of this book will focus on how various sex-related topics can be discussed with children of different age levels in the Christian home. In this present chapter, however, let's talk about simple, basic guidelines which will help us do the best possible job to guide our sons and daughters in their growth toward manhood and womanhood.

Here are some suggestions:

(1) Establish a home climate that enhances rather than inhibits sex education.

(2) Be alert for teaching opportunities.

(3) Be prepared.

(4) Be sensitive.

(5) Don't fail to stress the uniqueness of the Christian message. Let's look at each of these in turn.

Establish a Climate for Sex Education

Whether we're aware of it or not, we emit sex education messages to our children from the earliest days of their infancy. A baby who is cuddled and spoken to with tenderness and love is receiving a type of sex education. An infant basks in the pleasurable sensations of being picked up, held closely and tucked into a cozy bed. He comes to understand how wonderful and comfortable it is to be close to another body as he is cradled in loving arms and stroked adoringly while he sucks at his mother's breast or drinks warm milk from a bottle. All of this is nonverbal communication, and the infant learns quickly that his body produces sensations of enjoyment. It is pleasant to be near someone. He finds that relating to other people makes him feel good and happy inside. Such a loving atmosphere provides a wonderful setting in which his development as a human being, including his sexual development, can take place.

A second aspect of the climate we should aim for in the home is one in which children can not only sense love being directed toward them, but one in which they can also see the object lesson of their parents' love for each other. Families and individuals vary in the amount of affection they display through hugs, kisses and words of endearment. Some people are demonstrative; others (whose love may be just as deep) are not. Love can be shown in different ways, but the important thing is that it be shown.

A child learns a great deal by watching how his mother and father relate to one another. He can sense more than they realize how they feel about each other, their delight in one another (or lack of it), their devotion to each other, their concern, affection and enjoyment of one another's companionship.

A mother and father can illustrate to the child the warmth and depth that is possible in the relationship between a man and a woman. Children see the smile of understanding that passes between a husband and wife, the kiss as they greet one another or say goodbye, the spontaneous embraces when they're together, the quick squeeze of a hand or affectionate pat on the head. All this and more conveys to children what it really means for parents to love and respect each other. And this is a crucial part of sex education. Children may joke and tease about how silly it is to be "mushy" and "gushy," but underneath they are happy in the security of knowing their mom and dad really care about each other. "You don't know how lucky you are," a high school friend told a girl from a Christian home. "*Your* parents really love each other! So many parents don't."

A third requirement for developing a positive sex education in the home is openness. This means from earliest years, children are encouraged to feel at ease in talking with their parents about anything and everything that concerns them. It means parents will attempt to understand the child's point of view, taking time to listen carefully without stifling his honest expression of feelings.

Openness includes a willingness to learn and grow with our youngsters, rather than trying to pretend we know everything and have all the answers. It means being willing to admit that we're wrong sometimes. And it means being willing to say, "I'm sorry," to apologize and to ask forgiveness of our children when we've been wrong in a judgment. It also means accepting our children when they express ideas different than our own.

Openness means being free from pretense and hypocrisy and sincerely sharing our thoughts and feelings. It means not speaking one way to our children and living out our lives by a different standard.

In this kind of atmosphere, children will feel free to bring us their questions, doubts and problems without fear of censure and condemnation. Children don't want to be shamed, ridiculed, or chided. Children are people. They need affection and acceptance if their feelings and questionings are to be drawn out.

These then are the ingredients that produce an atmosphere where sex education can be communicated in an honest, natural and free manner. But a suitable home climate is only the beginning. Let's move on to some additional guidelines.

Be Alert for Teaching Opportunities

A good teacher doesn't see his task merely in terms of sitting by and waiting until questions are asked. Rather, he tries to stimulate wonder and curiosity so that questions *will* be asked. He wants to do more than just impart information. He wants to help each pupil become a learning, growing person who eagerly explores the wonderful world in which he lives. A good teacher knows that learning occurs gradually. Adaptations must be made to a child's interests, age level, and his capabilities to understand and assimilate information.

As teachers of sex education in the home, parents must also keep these things in mind. During the earliest years of a child's life, parents should be prepared to answer "Where did I come from?" in simple terms. Some children may not ask questions, or may stop asking them as they grow older. We are neglecting our responsibilities as sex educators if we say nothing. We have the responsibility to bring up the subject.

There are many concepts we want to share with our children. In the question of knowing God, we don't let them drift in the hope that some day they'll ask a question, or will find God for themselves. As Christian parents, we want very much to share our faith with our children during their earliest years. "Look at the beautiful butterfly God made," we say. Or, "God loves us very much, He helps and takes care of us," or "Jesus loves little children and we can talk to Him whenever we want." Or we explain that God wants us to love and be kind to other people.

Christian parents are unlikely to say, "We won't discuss God or the Bible. We'll sit back and wait for our children to take the initiative to ask us who God is. It isn't up to us to start conversation on such matters. They're too special and sacred. We'll wait."

On the contrary, Christians talk over the important concepts of God, faith and salvation with their children. Why then should sex be an isolated subject, packaged and locked up on a shelf marked, "Don't touch." If we view sex as a created gift of God, with provided guidance in His Word, why should we be hesitant about discussing sex with our sons and daughters? This doesn't mean, of course, that we rush out to present a lesson on the science of embryology to a three-year-old! But it does mean a foundation can be laid in the early years, with building blocks of knowledge added as the child grows older and his understanding expands.

Books written for specific age levels can be helpful in this area. More often, the child's own questions and interest will show us when he is ready for certain information. And we need to provide only as much information as the child needs at a particular time. He doesn't need a detailed explanation. This only confuses and frightens. He needs rather a simple answer to satisfy his curiosity.

For example, a two-year-old might notice his new baby sister doesn't have a penis. "Why?" he asks. Without making an issue of it, his mother may simply reply, "Because God made girls' bodies one way and boys' bodies another way. Little boys become daddies when they grow up, and little girls become mommies. That's why God made different kinds of bodies for men and women."

Obviously, such an answer would not be adequate for an older child. But for a young child, it can provide a foundation. This statement gives no false impressions and does not deny the association of the genital organs with urination (something the child is very much aware of by his own observation). An emphasis is given to God's design and plan, and attention is subtly drawn to the body parts that have something to do with "becoming a mommy or daddy." In other words, they are associated with sex and reproduction. A small child is, of course, catching only the tiniest hint of this, but the groundwork for later sex information is being laid.

But how can we bring up the subject of sex when our youngsters fail to ask questions? If we look for them, we'll find opportunities all around us. This is why developing a special sense of alertness is important. For example, ten-year-old Doug came home from school one day and announced he had heard a new joke from his friends. (The riddle asked, "How can you tell when a typewriter is pregnant?" The answer: "When it starts skipping periods.") Rather than scold him for telling the joke, or ignoring it, his mother realized that it might provide an excellent springboard for discussion. Did Doug understand that periods refer to menstrual periods that cease when a woman becomes pregnant? Doug's mother found there was some fuzzy thinking in her son's mind and he welcomed an opportunity to discuss the subject with her in a natural, casual manner.

Several months later without embarrassment the subject came up again. On this occasion, Doug said that his science teacher had shown a film on reproduction as part of a study unit on the human body. "It talked about what you told me about, Mom," he said. "By the way, what do you call it again when girls have bleeding every month?"

"Menstruation," his mother replied.

"Yes, that's it," said Doug. "The movie said girls about my age will begin to menstruate once every twenty-eight days or so. But how old are girls when it stops?"

"It doesn't just happen to *girls*, does it?" said Doug's older brother as he entered the room and broke into their conversation. "It still happens to grown women like you, too, doesn't it, Mom?" Their mother said yes and explained further because it was a teaching opportunity that shouldn't be missed. Doug's mother asked her boys if they would like to see what a woman wears to take care of the flow during her menstrual period. Curious, both boys looked with interest at the sanitary napkin, belt, and tampon their mother displayed in a kind of impromptu "show and tell."

Carefully she explained the external and internal

41

methods of protection. Their curiosity satisfied, the boys soon began talking about other events of the day. Once more, without embarrassment, sex education had been worked into the normal pattern of family life and conversation with ease and naturalness.

Opportunities to discuss sex can easily be found if a parent is willing to seize upon them. Many parents, of course, do not recognize or take advantage of opportunities when they come. Their failure to do so is unfortunate and regrettable. Their children are being deprived of knowledge they desperately need in order to handle the great exposure to sex given them via mass media.

Twelve-year-old Janet, for example, wondered about an advertisement for contraceptive foam she noticed in a magazine. When she asked her mother what it was, her mother flushed and sputtered that she hadn't the slightest idea. Then said curtly, "Twelve-year-old girls don't need to know about such things." Janet felt as though she had been slapped. An opportunity was missed, and a further step was taken toward the breakdown of parental and teen-age communication.

Often questions about sex are raised in a child's mind by things he hears on the radio, reads, or sees on TV or in movies. And these are often extremely difficult questions for parents to deal with. But evading them does not help the child. Kenny's father felt a bit nervous as he discussed with his son the dismissal of a male school teacher who had been accused of sodomy, but he knew the matter must be faced. It was better that he be the one to discuss it with Ken instead of letting the boy try to put the information together from scanty newspaper reports and gossip of his school friends.

In another family, an evening news report of the tragic rape and murder of a small girl on her way home from school provided opening conversation about sex as the family sat at dinner. Cheryl, the red-haired third-grader of the family, listened with fear and interest to the radio announcer before her father turned off the radio for the table grace. But as soon as her father said amen, Cheryl piped up and asked, "What's rape, Daddy?" Her parents had anticipated the question and guided Cheryl to a wise understanding.

For the Smiths, an opportunity for sex education arose unexpectedly as they passed a drive-in theater showing an X-rated movie. As their car drove past, the Smiths caught a glimpse of a vivid scene of sexual intercourse. "Look, Mom and Dad!" shouted seven-year-old Kathy. "Those people don't have any clothes on! What are they doing?" The older children giggled and turned their heads to watch as the car drove down the highway. It wasn't an easy moment for mom and dad! But to avoid the subject wouldn't have helped their children. With a quick silent prayer for courage and wisdom, Mr. and Mrs. Smith tried to describe simply what God intended the sexual embrace to be. And because many people choose not to follow God's way, they abuse and misuse something God intended to be a good gift for husbands and wives.

The occasions that give rise to sex education opportunities in these days are endless. If we refuse or neglect these opportunities, we are failing our children in one of the most important and sacred of all parental responsibilities.

Be Prepared

This motto, "Be Prepared," is not only for Girl Scouts and Boy Scouts. It's good advice for everyone. The book you are reading is an attempt to aid parents in this regard. The latter half deals with questions that most often arouse a child's curiosity. By reading this section in advance you will keep well ahead of your children and go a long way toward preventing the panic of unpreparedness.

It is also wise to purchase books that children themselves can read, or that you can read to them. For example, the colorful small book, *The Story of You,*[1] with its simple text and pictures drawn by children, can be a delightful bedtime story for a five-year-old. It describes his parents' love for each other and his own entrance into the world. Adding a Christian perspective to this subject is the Concordia Sex Education Series,[2] much acclaimed age-graded program for homes and churches. Also available are filmstrips, records and books to guide parents and group leaders.

Another outstanding series is the Life Cycle Library,[3] promoted by educators associated with *Weekly Reader,* an educational paper widely used in public schools. One important feature of these books is their wide use of pictures to explain how our bodies work and how babies develop and are born.

The sketches and diagrams in good sex education books are done tastefully, and only the most prudish mind would consider them pornographic or obscene. They picture a tiny sperm and ovum, a boy's and girl's sex organs, how conception takes place as the sperm and ovum meet, and how a woman's body changes during pregnancy. They do *not* show couples having sexual intercourse. A listing of better sex education books can be found in the back of this book.

Another aspect of preparation is making sure we know (and use) correct terminology with regard to sex-related topics. You don't need to be unreasonably detailed in this regard, citing every minute technical term and burdening tiny children with the vocabulary of a physiology textbook. But there's no reason, for example, that a male toddler, who points to various parts of his body and hears his parents say, "nose," "eye," "hand," "toe," should suddenly hear strange euphemisms when he points to his genital area and hear "pee-pee," "pee-wee," "wienie," "teapot," "periwinkle," to cite only a few. The correct name, of course, is *penis,* and the saclike structure under it is the *scrotum* and contains his *testicles.*

In females, the corresponding external genital area is the *vulva.* This is the entire area that includes the clitoris, the folds of skin surrounding it, and the openings to the urethra (out of which urine passes) and to the vagina (the passageway out of which the menstrual flow passes and through which babies pass during childbirth. It is the part of a woman's body which receives her husband's penis during sexual intercourse).

Correct terminology is also important in avoiding inaccurate impressions. For example, a baby does *not* grow in his mother's "tummy." Reproduction is not part of the stomach or digestive system. Rather, a baby grows in a special place inside the mother, a place called the *uterus.* Before leaving the subject of preparedness, one other matter should be mentioned—the importance of involving *both* parents in the discussion of sex-related topics.

Often a father or mother errs when they assume their children wouldn't be interested in discussing a sex problem. Tim Gray found this out one day as he and his son Jerry planted shrubs together. Always interested in Jerry's school subjects and activities, Mr. Gray asked how the recently organized debate club was coming along.

"Well," said Jerry, "we can't decide on a good topic yet. Our teacher and the class have suggested all sorts of subjects—war, drugs, poverty. But there's only one topic the whole class agrees on, and I don't know if we'll debate it. Mrs. Stevens is afraid some of the parents might object."

"What is the topic, Jerry?" asked his father.

Jerry put his foot on the shovel and gave it a hard push. "It's about whether or not abortion should be legalized."

Mr. Gray tried not to show his surprise. When he had been in the sixth grade, he had never even heard the word "abortion," and didn't have the slightest idea what it meant. But it was foolish, he thought, to deny or try to run away from the responsibility and new openness about sex in society. Besides, it was a subject Mr. Gray had thought about and was prepared to discuss with his son.

But many fathers and mothers are not prepared. Sociologist John Gagnon cites studies showing little change during this past century in the pattern of sex education. As children are growing up, sex information is gleaned piecemeal from peers. In approximately one half of all cases in studies cited by Gagnon, neither mother nor father provided sex information. In instances where sex education did occur in the home, it was far more likely to have been the mother, not the father who provided information. "The myth of the good heart-to-heart talk between father and son seems to be exactly that," writes Gagnon.[4]

This is regrettable. And particularly so in the Christian home. The Scriptures make clear that both fathers and mothers share the important responsibility of teaching and training the children God has placed in their charge. The book of Proverbs, for example, is full of admonitions which show how important this is. "Hear, my son, your father's instruction, and reject not your mother's teaching; for they are a fair garland for your head, and pendants for your neck" (Proverbs 1:8,9). Such passages addressed to children are meaningless unless their fathers and mothers are willing to face up to their responsibilities in *giving* them that instruction and teaching—including sex education.

46

Be Sensitive

Earlier, in the discussion on a home climate, we suggested a need for sensitivity and the importance of empathy and understanding, to grasp exactly what our child is asking about sex. What is it that troubles him? Are there hidden questions he hesitates to voice, but which make him anxious? Or is he just curious and seeking simple answers?

Sensitivity means trying to fit our answer to his age level. It means patience in answering what seems to be the same question asked over and over again, often in different forms and at different stages of a child's growth.

Sex education is gradual and involves much repetition. No child understands totally every bit of information he receives at a particular time. He absorbs only portions, depending on how much information he has had in the past, how mature his perception is of the world and his life at this point, and the setting in which he asks the question. Parents should not feel they failed to "get through" if a child repeats a question they thought they had explained adequately several months earlier. It probably means the child is ready for a deeper and broader look at the matter. Gradualness and repetition are part of learning in any subject. And the subject of sex is no different.

Our children need to grow little by little in sex knowledge, with each new layer of facts and insight placed on the strata underneath and resting on the foundation laid in earliest childhood.

Remembering our own childhood uncertainties will help us encourage our children to voice their honest concerns. As the Bible says, "The purpose in a man's mind is like deep water, but a man of understanding will draw it out" (Proverbs 20:5). Christian mothers and fathers need to be men and women "of understanding."

47

Another facet of sensitivity is listening to unspoken questions. Twelve-year-old Eric asked his dad if he or his mother had syphilis. Shocked and flustered, his father replied angrily, "What a terrible question for a kid to ask his father! What kind of people do you think your mother and I are? I never would have thought of saying such a thing to my dad when I was your age. Don't you think it's time you showed a little respect?"

Tears stung Eric's eyes, but he said nothing. And his dad made no further attempt to find out why his young son asked what he did. Actually, the question had arisen logically in Eric's mind when he ran across an article on venereal disease in a family magazine. The article said that syphilis could cause blindness, deafness and other serious problems to children of parents who had syphilis. The disease, the article pointed out, was contracted through sexual intercourse. Eric knew married couples had sex relations, and wondered if his parents might have contracted the disease from their intercourse. If so, thought Eric, the disease might be passed on to him! And it worried and frightened him that he might become blind or deaf.

All Eric was asking for from his father was reassurance. And if his father had been sensitive to his son's question he would have gently drawn out the real reason for the question. He could have explained to Eric that intercourse in itself doesn't cause syphilis, but rather the disease is passed on through promiscuity—through sex relations with persons outside the husband-wife relationship. The disease is spread through sexual contact with someone already infected with syphilis.

Eric could have been told that most states require blood tests to insure couples don't have the disease before they are permitted to marry and that husbands and wives who are faithful to each other never need worry about contracting the disease. Furthermore, the worries that troubled Eric referred specifically to *congenital* syphilis, the kind that infects a baby while he is developing inside a mother who is afflicted with the disease. Such a discussion with Eric could have been of great benefit in putting his mind at ease, as well as providing information on an important aspect of sex education—knowledge about venereal diseases.

Another family displayed sensitivity to the concern behind their child's question as they toured a museum. Impulsively, six-year-old Jeff ran up to a statue of a small nude boy and touched the stone penis. The museum guard glanced up, frowned, and walked toward Jeff. The guard reached Jeff just as his embarrassed parents pulled him away. They murmured their apologies and scolded Jeff for touching the displays. "I just had to touch it," said Jeff, "because I think all my friend's penises are like mine. But the penises on statues look different."

Jeff's problem was simply wondering if he was somehow different, maybe not normal. Jeff's father understood his son's problem and explained. "The little boy that you looked at," he said, "has a penis that wasn't circumcised. When you and most of your friends were tiny babies, you were circumcised. That's why your penis doesn't have that extra bit of skin around its tip like the statue does." This unembarrassed sensitivity shown by Jeff's father helped Jeff over his anxiety and reassured him that everything was normal.

In *Parents' Answer Book,* Dr. Charlotte del Solar tells about an insensitive parent who caused her twelve-year-old daughter great distress. Just after her first year of menstruation, the young girl asked her mother how a woman could know if she was pregnant. "A woman usually knows she is pregnant," said her mother, "because she misses her regular menstrual period." Terrified, the girl spent several weeks believing she was going to have a baby, even though she had never had sexual intercourse. Dr. del Solar pointed out that although the mother *heard* the girl's words, she didn't listen to the real question. Her mother failed to understand her daughter was speaking personally and needed reassurance.[5]

Don't Fail to Stress the
Uniqueness of the Christian Message

Although mentioned last, this guideline is most important in teaching children about sex. Children need to learn that God loves and cares. God understands the mysterious stirrings, worries and concerns that occur during adolescence. The Bible tells us "He remembers our frame" (Psalm 103:14). He knows how our bodies are made. He designed them!

Children can learn a sense of wonder in the knowledge of God's marvelous creation in their bodies. They can learn that God provides guidelines, gives comfort and has not abandoned them on a sea of sexual confusion.

Teen-agers, in their struggles with sexual temptation, can be helped by a realization that Jesus Christ understands, sympathizes and stands ready to help. Christ came into the world as a human being. He grew up just as our children grow up. He knows, not only as God, but also as man, what it means to go through the years of adolescence. Yet He did nothing to hinder His relationship with His heavenly Father. The Bible tells us that Jesus, although He never sinned, was tempted "in every respect," just as we are (Hebrews 4:15). God doesn't hold us accountable for temptations that come our way, but rather what we *do* in the face of temptation.

Teen-agers, aware of their own sexual struggles and temptations, sometimes wonder if Jesus ever faced similar tests. The Scriptures do not answer the question in specific terms, but there is no reason to think that Jesus did not experience such temptations. Why should we consider it worse for Him to have been tempted to break the seventh commandment ("You shall not commit adultery") than to be tempted to break the first commandment ("You shall have no other gods before me"), a commandment we *know* Satan tempted Him to transgress (Luke 4:5-8)? The important thing to remember is that He resisted temptation. He never sinned. But because He was tempted in the same way we are, He offers young people His understanding and resources. (See Hebrews 2:18.) They, too, can resist the "dazzling" allurements that pull them from God's will.

The following Scriptures help us understand that while we are responsible to God for our attitudes and conduct, He doesn't want to spoil our pleasure.

"For whatever God says to us is full of living power: it is sharper than the sharpest dagger, cutting swift and deep into our innermost thoughts and desires with all their parts, exposing us for what we really are. He knows about everyone, everywhere. Everything about us is bare and wide open to the all-seeing eyes of our living God; nothing can be hidden from him to whom we must explain all that we have done.

"But Jesus the Son of God is our great High Priest who has gone to heaven itself to help us; therefore let us never stop trusting him. This High Priest of ours understands our weaknesses, since he had the same temptations we do, though he never once gave way to them and sinned. So let us come boldly to the very throne of God and stay there to receive his mercy and to find grace to help us in our times of need" (Hebrews 4:12-16, *TLB*).

In helping our children learn about sex within a framework of the gospel message, we help them see the truth that God created sex, and the often unrecognized fact that God wants to guide and help us in this powerful and beautiful gift. We must further guide our children in the matter of God's view of sexual sin and the message of redemption. Young people sometimes stumble into sexual sins. When they do they often react with tremendous feelings of guilt. Some now believe God has cast them off and they can never be forgiven. Others react by thinking, "Well, I've already 'lost my virginity.' What does it matter what I do now? What have I got to lose?" Unfortunately some Christians add fuel to such reasoning with censure and condemnation. This harsh judgmental attitude implies that sex sins are somehow beyond the scope of God's forgiveness. But they are not. (See John 8:1-11 and Luke 7:36-50.)

Persons who have fallen into wrong sex relationships need to hear the *good news* that Christ came to bring. They need to know they are loved, welcomed, accepted. This does not mean that we condone sin, but it does mean we stress that the power of Jesus Christ is far greater than the power of sin. "The blood of Jesus his Son cleanses us from every sin. . . . If we confess our sins to him, he can be depended on to forgive us and to cleanse us from every wrong" (1 John 1:7,9, *TLB*). No person need feel he is forever doomed and made to suffer the pangs of guilt and remorse because he violated God's sexual standards during youth. If sin is confessed to God, it is immediately washed away—erased for eternity, because of the sacrificial death of our Saviour on the cross. Teen-agers, and everyone, can know it is possible to be restored and begin life anew. By personal faith in Christ, a person can live a life of victory over sin because of the dynamic power of Christ's resurrected life.

Let's Talk It Over

1. Mary and Ned told their teen-age daughters and eleven-year-old son they should feel free to come to either of them if they have questions about sex. Yet, the children never ask their parents. What is the reason for this? What more can Ned and Mary do to help their children learn about sex? Why isn't it enough to say to chil-

dren, "If you have questions about sex, just come to us"?

2. We have seen some important characteristics of a home climate that is conducive to healthy sex education. Now make a list of characteristics of a home that provides a *poor* climate for sex education. Think about your own childhood home, and then about your present home. How do their respective "climates" measure up?

3. Look back over the illustrations in this chapter which show ways parents might handle questions that arise. What are the mistakes made by some parents? What are some examples of handling sex education wisely? Can you think of similar instances that have occurred in rearing your own children?

4. Make a list of occasions in which there could have been excellent opportunities for sex education but which you failed to see at the time or else passed by. In what way could these have been used as springboards for discussion? If you had it to do over again, how would you now deal with each of these opportunities in the light of the guidelines presented in this chapter?

5. Why is it important to make every effort to present sex education within the context of the Christian message? What are some specific ways in which many Christian parents fail in this regard? Why does this happen, and how can it be remedied?

References

1. Edgar A. Cockefair and Ada Milam Cockefair, *The Story of You* (order direct from Monona Publications, P.O. Box 3222, Madison, Wisconsin 53704).

2. The Concordia Sex Education Series is published by the Concordia Publishing House, 3558 South Jefferson Ave., Saint Louis, Missouri 63118.

3. *The Life Cycle Library for Young People* (Chicago: Parent and Child Institute, 1969). For information, write to the Weekly Reader Family Book Service, Ameri-

can Education Publications, Education Center, Columbus, Ohio 43216.

4. John H. Gagnon, "Sexuality and Sexual Learning in the Child," in John H. Gagnon and William Simon, eds., *Sexual Deviance* (New York: Harper & Row, 1967), pp. 34,35.

5. Charlotte del Solar, Ph.D., *Parents' Answer Book* (Chicago: Parent and Child Institute, 1969), pp. 42,43. This book is part of the *Life Cycle Library* mentioned above.

CHAPTER FOUR

Helping Children
Develop a Christian Sex Ethic

Teaching children about sex is a two-sided task. There's the *factual* side—helping youngsters understand the difference between males and females. And there is the *moral* side—helping our children understand what's right and wrong in sex attitudes and behavior.

Most parents agree neither side of sex education is easy. But the area of moral standards seems to cause the most concern. Often parents feel if children and teens know too much about sex they'll want to put this knowledge into action and begin experimenting. The facts are quite the reverse. It's ignorance in sexual understanding, rather than accurate sex knowledge, that produces curiosity, experimentation and misguided conduct. Nevertheless, many parents still believe that what children don't know won't hurt them. And thus parents feel it's in the interest of *morality* to shield their children from knowledge of sexual *facts*.

There is no denying that teaching our children about morality is a challenging task. It always has been. From earliest times, man has had problems with right and wrong sexual behavior. Witness the many accounts of sex sins in the Bible. To many parents today's world seems worse than ever. We are bewildered by what we read and hear. We yearn desperately for our children to have high moral standards and steer clear of sexual involvements or practices that could "mess up" their lives. We want our children to be good. But what does the word "good" mean any more? It seems today's society provides little support to instill "old-fashioned virtues" in youth. There's a blurring of right and wrong. And because nothing seems clear-cut, it's tempting for parents to throw up their hands in despair and say, "What's the use? How can Christians stand in the face of the 'Playboy philosophy' and the 'new morality'?"

If you have wondered about this, don't give up. There's hope. Many of today's young people are surprisingly idealistic. They don't want to abandon themselves to a life of looseness and lewdness. They're not about to fling over every remnant of moral concern. Quite the contrary. They see the sham, hypocrisy and emptiness in the adult world, including marriage and sex, and often look for something better. As part of their search, they raise questions about traditional approaches to morality, and ask questions our generation never dared ask. And as responsible parents we must listen. If we don't, we won't be able to understand or guide them.

As our children search and begin to form a Christian sex code, we parents must keep three important areas in mind. First: Be aware of current trends and contemporary thinking. Second: See clearly the great responsibility God has given us to help our children find their way through a maze of conflicting standards and sexual confusion. Third: Search the Scriptures to find what God has to say about sex.

What's Going on These Days?

A mother of four daughters wrote to "Dear Abby" and expressed dismay over a letter from another mother who decided the surest way to have peace of mind was to give her sixteen-year-old daughter the "Pill". Never would *she* do such a thing, said the mother of four. That would be telling her girls to have sex relations! But she went on to say that if there were a form of oral contraceptive that could be purchased as a tasteless powder, she'd rush right out to buy it and sneak it into her daughters' breakfast cereal! She signed her letter, "Realist."[1]

Such a letter sums up a great deal about current sex trends and illustrates the inconsistency and confusion about moral values. It reminds us that one of the traditional arguments for premarital sexual abstinence (the fear of pregnancy) is losing strength. It further shows that some parents feel it is too difficult, if not impossible, to instill moral values in young people that would help them resist the pressures of a sex-worshiping society.

No More Hush-Hush

A quick look at our women's and family magazines illustrates the high degree of our society's preoccupation with sex. It isn't unusual to find articles in which parents debate whether it's wise or not to give their children contraceptives during teen-age dating days, or articles in which parents say they can't make up their minds about what's moral or immoral. There are articles in which young wives tell why they're glad they had premarital sex. And there are contrasting articles by other young wives in which they tell why they're glad they waited for marriage. Magazines and newspapers carry features on homosexuality, frigidity, wife-swapping, trial and group marriages, and abortion.

There is unprecedented freedom to talk about sex on television and radio. Not only is this true of talk shows, films and documentaries, but it's evident in advertising. Some people call it the sexual sell, "sexploitation," or "sexcess," but whatever it is, advertisers are convinced products are noticed and sell better if they're wrapped in sexy packaging. Products are said to be the means of getting guys to kiss girls, or of getting girls to chase guys.

Even young children pick up songs and slogans and go around talking about having "sex appeal." The most disturbing thing about this is that the worth of a person is measured in terms of his sex appeal, and that sex appeal is achieved by using a certain mouth wash, perfume, shaving lotion, or deodorant, or buying a particular car.

Modern song lyrics often have decidedly sexual meanings. This is by no means *always* the case. Many songs speak of romantic love and broken hearts similar to the popular songs parents remember from their own youth. Other songs speak of love in the broader sense of human brotherhood and peace, while others reflect the idealism of the young in seeking meaningful relationships and a warm, loving married life. Yet, there are other songs that speak of spending the night together, "going all the way," and hint at sensual meanings and sexual invitations. One song in recent years spoke of an affair between a married man and another woman in which the man declared that if such love is wrong, he wouldn't *want* to be right!

It would be good for parents to listen to these songs. Doing so would provide understanding about the kinds of sex messages young people are being exposed to and the stimuli that mold their ideas and attitudes.

The same is true for movies. Both modern cinema and live theater deal with themes that would have been taboo a decade ago. If you don't choose to see examples of such films, at least take time to read the reviews and become aware of what today's youth are seeing. Many modern movies are sensational and have little purpose beyond providing vicarious sexual thrills. On the other hand, there are serious films that treat sexual matters in ways that show abuses and misuses of sex in modern society. Others show the exploitation of women, the games men and women play as they manipulate and use one another, and the utter emptiness and meaninglessness of a life given over to sexual idolatry. Sadly, few movies present a positive, beautiful side of sex, love and marriage as intended by God.

The fact can't be denied that for many youth, movies are a prime means of sex education. Obviously, much of the mystery of sex disappears when it is portrayed in living color on the wide screen. Certain subtle messages about *values* come through as well as basic facts. Ideas like "it's OK to go to bed if you love each other," "sex is a normal, expected part of dating; everybody's doing it" or "sex is a great means of communication. So what if the couple just met and don't know each other's last names? They can get acquainted in bed, on the beach, or in the back seat of a car!"

It's foolish for parents to ignore the force of sex influence from movies or to fume, fuss and wish for more controls and censorship. The openness with which sex is discussed in our society is here to stay. As parents who want to teach sex from a Christian perspective, we must take time to understand the ideas that come to our youngsters and be prepared to discuss them openly and honestly in the light of our Christian faith.

What is true of movies applies to books our children read. Modern novels are quite explicit about sex. And it isn't unusual for such books to be included in the junior high and high school curricula. One eighth-grader told his mother about a scene in a book he was reading for an English class, in which a soldier engaged in sexual intercourse was shot. "Oh, it was awful," said the boy, "because they killed him while he was still inside the girl. And she had to find a way to get out of that place fast! There was shooting all around her." "How different from my eighth-grade reading," thought the mother. "Our requirements included *Lassie Come Home, Tom Sawyer,* and *Hans Brinker!*" However, it was the war situation that captured the boy's attention, not the sex. It was for the overall story that the book had been included in the English curricula. It was incidental that there were explicit sex scenes in this book, as well as in other books. But many teachers feel they should not exclude a well-written novel because it describes a sex scene in a particular chapter.

Again, as in the case of songs and movies, parents should find out what books their pre-teens and teenagers are reading for their courses in school and become aware of any misconceptions young people may be getting in their sex education. Be prepared to discuss it with them. Also, take advantage of the factual knowledge that comes across in some of these books, and use it as a springboard for talking over that particular aspect of sex. You may be surprised to find that often your youngster really isn't interested only in the parts that talk about sex. He'd rather read the whole story.

Instead of complaining that sex is no longer given the silent treatment, let's take advantage of the openness and communicate with our children. Help them handle the things they're learning. Above all, let's not be *afraid* of the world in which our children are growing up. Let us remember God is with us, just as He has been with His people down through the ages. No problem is too great for Him and no challenge too great for us when He is with us.

No Consensus on Sex Standards

One of the characteristics of our time is sexual openness. Another is lack of agreement about what is right and wrong with contemporary sexual morality.

In a society where most citizens agree on a prescribed behavior, and where the society's government, schools

60

and churches support that position, children quickly grasp the norm for accepted conduct.

In the United States most agree that stealing and murder are wrong. Children learn early from parents, teachers, laws and mass media that it's not right to kill or take something that belongs to someone else.

However, today's sexual morality enjoys little of this consensus and this is where the confusion comes in. Parents are conditioned to think of sexual behavior in terms of *timing*. Sex before the wedding is wrong; sex after the wedding is right. It's as simple as that.

"No, it isn't as simple as that," claims the younger generation. "It's not the *when* but the *why* that's important. It's *meaning*, not timing, that matters."

They point out there are vast differences in the kinds of sexual encounters that may take place before marriage, and they wonder how they can all be lumped into the same category. There's the man, for example, who thinks of a woman as a sex object to use for his personal gratification, only to toss her aside afterwards as though she were a paper cup.

There's also the girl who is eager to bed down with every male she dates. "We agree this is wrong," cry the voices of modern youth.

"But what about the engaged couple who want to express their love sexually the night before overseas military service parts them for a year? Isn't it fair to say that sex for this couple is different than for a person sleeping with a prostitute?" These questions are being asked by high school and college youth today, including young people from Christian homes. As parents, we need to understand this kind of reasoning before we can deal with it. Sex researcher and sociologist Ira Reiss points out that modern young people feel sex codes and life styles should be chosen to fit the individual's personality. They are not asking for an "anything goes" attitude toward sex. They feel a person should be free to make a personal choice from among several different sex standards. Professor Reiss says that youth today tend to feel that the choice of a sex code, political party, or religion are matters that should be left up to the individual.[2]

In his book, *Premarital Sexual Standards in America,* Dr. Reiss cites four different popular views on sexual morality.[3] His research shows some persons believe in the "double standard." Such a person feels premarital sex is fine for men but not for women. They excuse men on the grounds that "boys will be boys" and that it's only "natural" for them to "sow wild oats." Persons who accept the double standard often believe that men have greater sexual drives and desire for release than do women. Men who hold such views don't hesitate to have sexual intercourse with a variety of women, but insist they'll marry only a virgin.

Sex-just-for-the-fun-of-it is another approach to the question of sexual conduct before marriage. Those who believe this feel men *and* women should be free to have premarital sex as part of the adventure of dating. Being serious about each other doesn't matter, nor does it matter if they don't know each other well. All they want is warm bodies and fun for the moment. This is a tenet of the "Playboy philosophy."

Others feel this destroys the beauty of sex, making it a mechanical act, a momentary thrill, and separating it from the context of love and commitment. The premarital standard of sex-just-for-the-fun-of-it exploits individuals as a thing or toy, as does the double standard. The only difference is that in the double standard, the man does the exploiting. In the other standard, *both* partners use each other. Those who criticize these standards point out that both emphasize sex as being "body-centered" rather than "person-centered."

OK. What do critics of these two standards suggest in

their place? Some say sex must be linked with love. Others say it must be love plus marriage. Dr. Reiss finds these two views summarize the most popular view of sex in America today.

Those who say, "Love makes it OK," believe that men and women have the right to engage in sexual intercourse before marriage *provided* there is a serious relationship involved. The couple must feel some commitment to one another. That is, going steady, being engaged, or very serious. "Their deep affection for each other makes sexual expression of their love permissible," say adherents of this view. "And even if they break up, at least they have confined their copulation only *to each other* during the time they were serious."

Aware of the pitfalls of this, others say the traditional standard of total sexual abstinence before marriage is the only accepted standard. This is consistent with the teachings given to the people of God in the Old and New Testaments. It also has been the official view of our society. However, the attitudes of young people today seem to indicate a movement from the standard "save sex until marriage" to "sex may be right if two persons are in love."

Is There Really a Sex Revolution Today?

Many authorities feel the word "evolution" is more appropriate than "revolution." Contrary to popular belief most traditional values are being continued. "If there has been a sex *revolution*," say some researchers, "it occurred after World War I during the roaring twenties." It was then many young persons rebelled against the sexual attitudes of the Victorian age.

Studies show that during the nineteenth century, approximately a fourth of all brides were not virgins. And during the 1920's, this jumped to fifty percent. According to Dr. Reiss, the rate has remained much the same from

63

the 1920's to the present time. Dr. Reiss, however, predicts the rate *may* jump another ten percent during the present decade.[4] The rate of premarital sex among men is somewhat higher. It ranges to over ninety percent for those with least education to about seventy percent with college education.[5]

Of course, in speaking of rates of permarital intercourse, we're speaking in terms of *percentages,* not actual numbers. In terms of actual numbers, there *are* more sexually experienced young people today—simply because the population has grown and more young people are alive at this particular time (due to the post-World War II "baby boom"). Even if the *percentage* of those engaging in premarital sex is little different than that characterizing youth of the 1920's, the actual number of young men and women who are sexually active is much greater.

Perhaps this sounds complicated, and you wonder what it has to do with sex education in the Christian home. Simply this. It shows us a true picture of today's sexual conduct and behavior and helps us avoid statements like, "This generation is corrupt. All they think about is sex. Why, when I was a boy. . . ."

But why does it seem worse now? For one thing, people talk about it more. Sex isn't the hushed-up subject it used to be because the mass media keep us well informed. This doesn't mean, however, that no changes have taken place. For one thing, there has been a movement away from the "double standard." Women are now looked upon as having sexual needs and rights just as men do.[6] Many young people of both sexes feel a loving relationship is necessary before sex comes into the picture, although more women than men feel this way. Even in this, things may be changing, however.[7]

This is not to say things are getting better. The point is we must understand the kinds of changes that are taking place in today's world. One of the biggest changes is how to handle guilt. If dad or grandpa had premarital sex, he felt guilty that he had done wrong, had sinned, or at least had broken society's moral code. The couple who "had to get married" were frowned upon with deep social disapproval. An unwed mother was a shocking disgrace. And girls who married in white gowns were expected to be virgins.

The modern generation, however, feels differently. Maybe actual behavior hasn't changed that much. But attitudes have. Thus, many modern teen-agers and young adults tend to rationalize their premarital sexual behavior. They are not convinced it is necessarily always wrong; and because of this, are less apt to feel guilty.

The contemporary attitude about premarital sex is difficult for many parents to understand. The following illustration may help make the picture clearer.

Suppose you are riding in the family car with your newly licensed teen-age son. As you approach an intersection, the light turns red, but your son continues to drive through. Shaken, you say, "Bill, do you realize what you just did? You went through a red light! You've violated a traffic law. Don't you know rules like that are made for our good and it's dangerous to ignore them?" Bill is sorry and sheepishly apologizes.

Now suppose after a long absence on business in a distant country you again climb into the car with your son. Again, he goes through a red light, and another, and still another. You wonder if Bill is color-blind. It's hard to scold him after being away so long, but finally you can't keep quiet. "Bill! You just went through a red light. You broke a law!" The boy replies, "No, I didn't." "But, but," you stammer, "I saw you! You went through a red light —in fact, several." "I know," says Bill. "But you just denied it!" you exclaim. "No, I didn't deny I went through a red light," replies Bill. "I deny that I broke a law!

Haven't you noticed the other cars? The *rules* have been changed. Visual researchers discovered that the colors should be reversed. Green is better for stopping and red is less a warning color than people think. Even our car's taillights are green. So you're right. I did go through a red light. But I didn't do anything wrong. We now have a whole new system of rules."

This is the way many young people think about premarital sex behavior. The old rules said that sex before marriage was wrong. Although people went ahead and did it anyway (went through the "stop light"), they knew they were breaking a rule. Under some of the new sex standards and under certain conditions, premarital sex is not seen to be wrong. Many young moderns are convinced that the rules have been changed. That when two persons in love engage in premarital intercourse they are not driving through a "stop light" but are proceeding on a journey where there are altogether different rules. The new rules are *fairness* (no exploitation), *equality* (what's right for boys is also right for girls), *responsibility* (taking precautions to avoid pregnancy and venereal disease), and *appropriateness* (do the persons really feel a love and commitment toward each other?).

This entire discussion has, of course, left out the question of moral absolutes. Namely, the eternal, unchanging law of God which has much to say about sexual conduct. We will discuss some of these concepts later. For now, we must continue with an overview of what's going on in today's sexual scene. Hopefully it will help parents see the new kind of reasoning that characterizes many youthful minds.

Changing Definitions

In a book designed to guide medical doctors in dealing with adolescent needs and problems, there appears the following illustration:

"The parents of a 16-year-old girl returned home unexpectedly and found the daughter and her 18-year-old boyfriend engaged in mutual oral-genital sexual activity. During the tempestuous period that followed, the girl admitted the practice had been frequent for several months and screamed at her parents, 'You ought to be glad—at least I can't get pregnant.' "[8]

This story serves to illustrate something that parents may find disconcerting. Not only do many today feel that the *rules* have been changed, they also feel that new *definitions* are in order. Let's look at two examples—chastity and obscenity.

The story of the 16-year-old and her extremely intimate petting with her boyfriend is an example of how large numbers of modern youth have found a way to "preserve virginity" and obtain sexual gratification at the same time. They have decided "chastity," "virginity," and "saving until marriage" means never engaging in full intercourse. A person may have engaged in all the techniques of marital foreplay but he or she is convinced this is *not* premarital sex, even though orgasm may have taken place.

Obscenity is another word that has changed meaning in the minds of many contemporary young people. They see sex as something natural, beautiful and certainly not "obscene," even when it's referred to in four-letter words. You've probably heard statements like: "What's obscene about spending the night with someone you love? That's not obscene; sex is beautiful! I'll tell you what's obscene. It's obscene to kill and maim babies in a senseless war. It's obscene to let people live in squalor and malnutrition in the richest nation in the world. Those are the kinds of things that are 'obscene'—not sex."

Actually, young people have something to say to us in this regard; not only through their concern for social is-

67

sues, but in their vision of sex as something natural and beautiful. True, we see errors in some of their reasoning about when, where, and with whom sexual expression is appropriate. But there is something healthy about the refusal of this generation to accept the old idea that "sex is dirty." Where did the idea that sex is dirty ever come from? Possibly it originated because of the location of sex organs and the association of this with waste removal. The idea of odor and mess may have bothered some people, especially in the days before hygienic cleanliness was emphasized and sex was tied to people's minds with excretion. It's still common to refer to a baby's act of moving his bowels as "he dirtied himself," or "he dirtied his diaper."

As we saw earlier, pagan ideas about the body's "evil" had an influence on certain early church leaders. Such men voiced repugnance at the idea that human beings are born from an opening that lies between the openings for urination and intestinal discharge. They were further appalled to think of the other fluids within the human body. They spoke with revulsion of such things as phlegm, saliva, blood, and masticated food. The aversion felt by some was so great they spoke of women's sexual organs as "sewers."

There is also another possibility. Our word "obscene" comes from the Latin adjective *obscenus,* which can mean: "filthy," "indecent," or "ominous." The ancient Romans evidently coined the word from another Latin word, *caenum* which means "mud" or "filth."

The three meanings of *obscenus* illustrate an interesting anthropological fact found among primitive tribes. From earliest times, human cultures and religions have strangely related "unclean" and "holy." Human blood, for example, may be regarded as sacred. But a menstruating woman is considered "unclean." Taboos about sexual functions among pre-literate tribes often show this strange inconsistency. Sex, because it is viewed as a strange power that brings new lives into the world, is unspeakably sacred and surrounded with rituals and rules. On the other hand, because this is such a powerful force, sex is often seen to be something dangerous and defiling. Some ethnic cultures believe sexual intercourse makes a couple "unclean" and requires ceremonial washings. In one tribe, a woman must wash both her husband and herself after copulation. If she doesn't, it is thought the man will fall ill when his wife cooks for him in such an "unclean" state. Furthermore, she must keep the pot she uses to wash herself well hidden. If she doesn't, an unsuspecting man may stumble over it and lose his virility.[9]

The idea of sex being "filthy" then could relate to primitive ideas about sex as "ominous," mysterious and sacred.

The third meaning of *obscenus,* "indecent," would then refer to persons who acted out-of-order with the society's norm. One thing is certain, today's young people are free from superstitions that sex is filthy and is surrounded by mystique and magic. They live in a scientific age and understand the workings of the human body.

This doesn't mean all sense of "mystery" is gone or that sex has become commonplace. It means the *ignorance* that caused people to be afraid and ashamed of their bodies is a lesser problem for today's youth.

This is illustrated in an article that told of an eighth-grader who watched a sex education film with amazement as he saw a sperm and egg unite to form the beginning of a baby. "I can't believe it," said the boy. "That doesn't sound dirty at all."[10] Parents who truly want to keep the doors of communication open with their offspring should keep this in mind. The human body and human sexuality spring not from the gutter, but from the hand of God.

Weakening of the Old
Arguments for Premarital Chastity

As parents look at present-day sexual morality, they are disturbed that many young people no longer listen to traditional reasons for saving sex for marriage. Many members of the "now generation" say, "Why wait? Who knows what tomorrow will bring? The whole world may be blown up! It's important to live life to the fullest right now. Why delay anything that promises pleasure?" This is not a new concept. The book of Ecclesiastes exposes the emptiness of the philosophy that said "Eat, drink, and be merry, for tomorrow we die."

When people ask their parents, church leaders and other adults why they should wait, traditional reasons are usually given: (1) "You might get pregnant" (or "get a girl pregnant"); (2) "You might catch a venereal disease"; (3) "You'll feel guilty and it will harm your mental health"; (4) "You'll ruin your chances of a happy marriage later on."

Most of these traditional reasons are now being challenged. "If sex before marriage is wrong *only* because of permarital pregnancy," say many of today's youth, "then let every girl use the pill."

"No!" shouts the adult world, "this would be wrong!" Or, "You might contract gonorrhea or syphilis."

"But," counters youth, "modern medicine has found ways to treat these diseases. Furthermore, they're working on a vaccine to immunize against VD. If science finds a way to conquer venereal diseases, *then* can we assume that sex before marriage is OK?"

Again there's a resounding "No" from the older generation. This time they say those who indulge will feel guilty. And young people counter with arguments from those who say they never feel guilty. That guilt comes only if one first thinks something is wrong and goes

70

against his conscience. But if a person is convinced pre-marital sex is permissible, there will be no guilt.

The older generation tries again, this time using the "unhappy marriage" argument. Again young moderns reply with handfuls of contradictory statistics. Some findings agree that premarital sex causes marital problems later. Others give evidence that premarital sexual experience has little effect on subsequent marital success. Such statistics show that many things must be considered, the young people say. With whom did one have premarital intercourse; with one's future marriage partner or someone else? Was there a variety of experiences with many different people? How often did it take place?

What can Christian parents say? Are there no answers for our young people? Of course there are. But our answers must be rooted in God's revelation—not in human arguments, which may change, topple and leave our children with nothing to hold on to. Youngsters, of course, should be warned about premarital pregnancy, venereal disease, and the risk of later marital unhappiness. But the point is, these arguments should not be the main reasons for citing high standards in sexual morality. Our Christian standards and way of life are based on commitment to Jesus Christ and a determination to know and do His perfect will. Which means there is a Christian view of sexual morality. And Christian parents have the solemn responsibility to teach their children what this is.

What Is Our Responsibility as Parents?

"Train up a child in the way he should go, and when he is old he will not depart from it" (Proverbs 22:6). All of us are familiar with this verse. Yet, when children of Christian parents go wrong they are confused. "We *thought* we were training our children in God's way," they say, "but the verse didn't come true for us. Our children departed from the way we taught them. Our only

71

consolation now is to hope someday when they're older, they'll return."

Other sympathetic parents wonder if this is the way it has to be. "Even if our children do return to God later in life," say some, "think of the wasted years. Why is it that young people from Christian families sometimes run away from home, use drugs, or set up housekeeping without getting married? Isn't there anything that can be done earlier in childhood to prevent this from happening?"

Let's try to answer this from Scripture. While it is true we live in a sinful world and temptations surround us, there are guidelines to help us make Proverbs 22:6 come true. Let's look at two important Scriptures.

"You shall love the Lord your God with all your heart, and with all your soul, and with all your might. And these words which I command you this day shall be upon your heart; and you shall teach them diligently to your children, and shall talk of them when you sit in your house, and when you walk by the way, and when you lie down, and when you rise. . . . You shall fear the Lord your God; you shall serve him, and swear by his name. You shall not go after other gods, of the gods of the peoples who are round about you; for the Lord your God in the midst of you is a jealous God. . . . When your son asks you in time to come, 'What is the meaning of the testimonies and the statutes and the ordinances which the Lord our God has commanded you?' then you shall say to your son, 'We were Pharaoh's slaves in Egypt; and the Lord brought us out of Egypt with a mighty hand. . . . And the Lord commanded us to do all these statutes, to fear the Lord our God, for our good always. . . .'" (Deuteronomy 6:5-7,13-15,20,21,24).

"My son, keep your father's commandment, and forsake not your mother's teaching. Bind them upon your heart always; tie them about your neck. When you walk, they will lead you; when you lie down, they will watch over you; and when you awake, they will talk with you. For the commandment is a lamp and the teaching a light, and the reproofs of discipline are the way of life, to preserve you from the evil woman, from the smooth tongue of the adventuress. Do not desire her beauty in your heart, and do not let her capture you with her eyelashes; for a harlot may be hired for a loaf of bread, but an adulteress stalks a man's very life. Can a man carry fire in his bosom and his clothes not be burned? Or can one walk upon hot coals and his feet not be scorched? . . . He who commits adultery has no sense; he who does it destroys himself" (Proverbs 6:20-28,32).

These two passages show three general principles for Christian parents to follow: (1) God expects us to share His Word and Himself with our children; (2) Parents must prepare children to live in *this* world—not utopia; (3) Parents are responsible for the moral education of their children.

God's Expectation

When God redeemed His people from Egyptian bondage, He asked them to love, serve, and fear Him (that is, to show reverence, awe, respect), to obey, and be loyal to Him. But that isn't all. The passage in Deuteronomy makes it clear that parents are to communicate these values to their children.

God tells His people to share His Word and His will with their children during the everyday routines of life. As the family sits at breakfast, as mother or father walk with their children outdoors, or in the cozy togetherness of bedtime. Any time, all the time, parents who love God are expected to guide their children in loving Him. God's words "written on the hearts" of parents, mean *knowledge* of His commands and a desire to *obey* them. Parents should not dismiss their responsibility, saying their own spiritual education is faulty. Nor should they turn over their children's spiritual education to institutions for religious instruction; i.e., church, Sunday School, or youth groups. Parents, according to Scripture, are responsible for teaching their children about God.

Furthermore, conversations about the Lord, His instructions and commands are not to be forced, cold, or formal. They are to occur naturally all through the day as evidences of His power—the world He created, the daily provision of food, the protection from injury. Such an atmosphere encourages children to *ask questions* about God and His purposes. And this is exactly what God expects and desires of His people. (See Deuteronomy 6:20 ff.)

Parents are to be prepared by thinking through these matters and being ready with answers. When a child in the Old Testament asked why God wanted them to obey His commandments, the parents were to call attention to what God had done for His people. He had delivered them from slavery. He had given them a new life. "And because God delivered our forefathers," said the parents, "we, out of love, want to follow and obey Him" (Deuteronomy 6:21-24).

Surely God expects as much of His people today! Christian parents should not take lightly their responsibility to bring up their children "in the discipline and instruction of the Lord" (Ephesians 6:4). This goes far deeper than attending public worship services. It means sharing God with our children every day of the week, every month of the year, and guiding them in a faith that is vital and dynamic. It means each Christian home should be a house of God, filled with His presence and radiant with His love.

Realistic Preparation

The people of Israel did *not* rear their children in anti-

74

septic surroundings. They were surrounded by nations and people that did not know, honor, nor obey the Lord. The idolatry of the ancient Near East was centered largely around fertility cults where people concerned themselves with productiveness for fields, livestock and human beings. Their worship was directed toward the gods and goddesses whom they felt controlled such processes. Not surprisingly, human sexuality was revered to the point of idolatrous worship.

Images of male and female genitals (especially those of the male) were carved from stone, wood or molded from clay and set up in places of pagan worship. It was not unusual to see carvings of nude men and women publicly displayed. Or clay figurines of rotund naked women with enormous hanging breasts and swollen pregnant abdomens. Pagan temples employed prostitutes who served as priestesses, with sexual acts considered as part of the ceremony. Some heathen sanctuaries had male prostitutes for homosexual practices.

The Israelites were strictly warned not to allow either type of prostitution to be associated with their worship of God. (See Deuteronomy 23:17,18.) They were also warned to have nothing to do with the *sexual orgies* that were performed as religious rites in honor of pagan deities.

In such a world as this, God asked His people to bring up their children in holiness and purity! Can we say the challenge He gives us today is more difficult? That our times are worse, or our task harder? Were the "good old days" of Bible times or any other yesteryear better days in which to rear children? No. Every age has its problems, evils and temptations. There has never been a time in which sex has not presented problems.

During the Victorian era in England when sex was hushed up, abuses abounded, adultery was prevalent, pornography flourished, and prostitution was at an all-time high. Nor is there any *place* where our children will be protected from sexual temptations and sin. Girls attending Christian colleges, as well as secular schools, have become pregnant out of wedlock. Boys attending reputable Christian camps have learned off-color stories from sons of missionaries attending the same camps. Persons active in gospel-preaching churches and organizations have become sexually involved in ways displeasing to God. As long as we are in this world, there is no place to escape sexual enticements and temptations. The ascetics of long ago, who lived atop pillars, in caves, or in deserts, discovered temptation went with them in their minds.

The only solid preparation and defense for ourselves and our children is listening to our Lord when He said, "I do not pray that thou shouldst take them out of the world, but that thou shouldst keep them from the evil one. They are not of the world, even as I am not of the world" (John 17:15,16).

In Deuteronomy, God said, "You shall not go after the gods of the people who are round about you. You are to remember the Lord your God in the midst of you." It is evident the world has goals, values and gods different than the Christian. And sex is not the least of these gods. But we must remember and convey to our children that God is in our midst. Paul tells us the same thing in 1 Corinthians 6:19 when he says, "your body is a temple of the Holy Spirit within you."

Realistic preparation for life in this world, then, includes helping our children understand what God has spoken and what He requires. It also includes knowing about the world in which our children are growing up and warning them, in specific ways, of its pitfalls. This doesn't mean we'll rear fearful, suspicious, prudish, distrustful paranoids. God's way is not one of bondage, but of freedom (Galatians 5:1). Knowing and obeying His

76

commands does not steal the joys of life; rather it means an exhilarating life filled with richness, meaning and purpose. Just as the Psalmist said, "I will keep thy law continually, for ever and ever; and I shall walk at liberty" (Psalm 119:44,45). We must help our children understand that doing God's will, though sometimes different than their peers, is not a tiresome chore.

Moral Education

There is a sad story in the Old Testament, of Eli, the priest, who cared for the child Samuel after he had been dedicated to the service of the Lord. But Eli had two sons who grew up to be selfish, greedy young men, unconcerned with obedience to the Lord. They cheated, lied, threatened violence, and blasphemed God (1 Samuel 2:12 ff.). Eli knew what they were doing, but he was an indulgent father and did nothing to stop them. God warned Eli that his failure to take action made him an accomplice in their crimes. It also meant Eli honored his children above God (1 Samuel 2:29).

And matters worsened. Eli's sons began having sex relations with the young women who served at the door of God's tabernacle. What a scandal! It seemed everyone in Israel was talking about the priest's sons. Word got back to Eli and he scolded his sons and warned them they were sinning against God. But it was too late. They were set in their ways and refused the counsel of their father. God told Eli that punishment and death would come to the family and the privilege of the priesthood would disappear from their lineage.

God's sad words to Eli have a message for all parents. "I tell him that I am about to punish his house for ever, for the iniquity which he knew, because his sons were blaspheming God, and he did not restrain them" (1 Samuel 3:13).

If we look at Proverbs 6, we see both mothers and fa-

77

thers are responsible for the spiritual instruction of their children. This instruction must include *doctrine* (knowledge about God, His character and His works) and *ethics* (knowledge about how we are to live as God's people in this world). It is wrong to shirk our responsibility in either area, because God holds this to be the parents' solemn trust.

If children learn Bible stories and facts, but never receive instruction about how these relate to their life, their Christian education is faulty. On the other hand, if all they are given to guide their behavior are rules, commandments, and "thou-shalt-nots," their spiritual education is just as faulty.

The passage in Proverbs 6:20 ff. bears a striking similarity to the passage in Deuteronomy. There the emphasis is on the parents' duty to continually teach their children the ways of the Lord. Now we see in Proverbs that the young person is expected to assimilate that teaching so it becomes *a part of him,* just as food does! (Often in Scripture God's words are compared to food—bread, honey, milk, meat.) It's at this point the young person will make God's truths workable concepts to guide, steady and keep him strong. When the time comes to be on his own, away from his parents' influence, he'll stand true to God's Word.

This includes following biblical teachings on sexual matters. Notice verses 23-32 of Proverbs 6. Here the emphasis is on a young man who might be seduced by an evil woman. But the passage should have as much meaning to a young woman who needs to be warned about the flatteries and seductive maneuvers of playboys like Eli's sons!

What Does the Bible Say About Sex Ethics?

It is never too early to share with our children the biblical ideal of sex and marriage. One way to do this is teach the Ten Commandments (Exodus 20). They can be rephrased so a very small child will understand. ("You shall not lie," "You shall not steal.") When it comes to the matter of the seventh commandment, "You shall not commit adultery," many parents hesitate. How do you explain this to a five-year-old? Books for children on the Ten Commandments seldom help. If anything, they rephrase it to "Thou shalt think pure thoughts," which still requires an explanation. In teaching this commandment to a young child it might be helpful to recast it as a positive statement. "Thou shalt," rather than a "Thou shalt not." For example, try, "You should want to please God in marriage." Then explain, "That means when you get married like Mommy and Daddy, God wants a husband and wife to love each other and their children in a very special way." Or try, "God wants mommies and daddies to love and belong only to each other." Or, "A man should not love another woman the way he loves his wife, and a woman should not love another man the way she loves her husband."

With this kind of groundwork, you can guide your child as he is exposed to mass media reports of adultery. For example, it is not uncommon in television dramas and movies for the hero to have an affair. "That man had *two* wives," said a first-grader after watching a TV film.

"No," said his parents, "Only the dark-haired lady was his wife. He just had a girlfriend he lived with sometimes. This man broke one of God's commandments," said his mother. "Do you know which one?"

"The one about pleasing God in marriage," replied the child.

"What that man did was *adultery*, wasn't it?" said his nine-year-old brother.

"Yes," said the mother, "and God says that's wrong."

An approach like this in a Christian home is better than avoiding or ignoring such matters. It is a practical way of applying the passages in Deuteronomy and Proverbs.

Another subject children can learn at an early age is the importance of Christians marrying only fellow-believers. A Christian who wants to please and serve Jesus, can never have a happy home if the husband or wife doesn't love Jesus. Husband and wife might love each other and their children, but they couldn't share every part of life if they don't share faith in Christ.

As the children grow older, wise parents will introduce Scriptures that support a Christian position of sexual morality. One passage is 1 Thessalonians 4:1-8 (*NEB*):

"And now, my friends, we have one thing to beg and pray of you, by our fellowship with the Lord Jesus. We passed on to you the tradition of the way we must live to please God; you are indeed already following it, but we beg you to do so yet more thoroughly.

"For you know what orders we gave you, in the name of the Lord Jesus. This is the will of God, that you should be holy: you must abstain from fornication; each one of you must learn to gain mastery over his body, to hallow and honour it, not giving way to lust like the pagans who are ignorant of God; and no man must do his brother wrong in this matter, or invade his rights, because, as we told you before with all emphasis, the Lord punishes all such offences.

"For God called us to holiness, not to impurity. Anyone therefore who flouts these rules is flouting, not man, but God who bestows upon you his Holy Spirit."

If you have teen-agers, this would be an excellent passage to discuss during family devotions. See if they can find the following six principles.

First, the principle of *commitment*. Paul tells these new Christians their former sex standards were lax. Paul emphasized his instructions and tells the Thessalonians they must now live to please God. He does not tell the

80

Thessalonian Christians to steer clear of premarital sex to avoid unwanted pregnancies, or venereal diseases. Rather, Paul says that God called them to holiness, not to impurity. And anyone who flouts these rules flouts, not man, but *God*. The person who commits his life to Christ must also hand over his sex life and ask for God's guidance and control.

Second, the passage makes clear the principle of *continence* or "abstaining from fornication." Which means unmarried persons should not engage in sexual intercourse. There is no equivocation here, no exceptions permitted. No, "but if we're in love," or "maybe if the couple is engaged." Abstinence from premarital sex is a clearly stated command of God.

Third, the principle of *control*. The Christian is told to "learn to gain mastery over his body." Sex desires are normal; they are not to be despised or denied. But he cannot permit sex to control him. He must be in charge of his passions and never permit them to be expressed in ways contrary to the will of God. (See also Romans 6:12,13.)

The principle of *contrast* is fourth. Because Christians base their attitudes and conduct on their commitment to Christ, it isn't surprising that Christian standards and behavior will be different from those who have not entered into a personal relationship with God. Paul spoke of this when he told the Thessalonian Christians their lives must show a definite change, and that they must now follow God's standard for sexual behavior. Persons "who are ignorant of God," says Paul, "give way to lust." Outside of Christ, they see no reason not to gratify their sexual urges and appetites. But not so the Christian. He must be different.

The fifth principle is *consideration*. In a real sense we *are* "our brother's keeper." We must always keep the rights and well-being of others in mind. Here the principle of neighbor-love comes into focus. The Christian must consider *others* who may be hurt or harmed if he pursues a course of selfish gratification. Jesus said the first and greatest commandment is to love God with our entire being. And it is in this perspective that the Christian's sex ethic must first be viewed. But Jesus said the second great commandment is "like unto it" and that is the commandment that one should love his neighbor as himself (Matthew 22:36-39). "Love does no wrong to a neighbor; therefore love is the fulfilling of the law" (Romans 13:10). In 1 Thessalonians, Paul applies this principle specifically to correct sex conduct. A Christian does not have the right to "use" somebody for his own sexual gratification, because all humans are made in the image of God. Such action "wrongs" a Christian brother or sister. In addition to hurting one's own body, premarital sex cheats on one's future spouse. As one teen-age girl said, "Aside from the issue of fornication, I feel having sex relations for me would be like committing adultery in advance. I would be unfaithful and hurting the man I'll someday marry. I want to keep myself for him."

Lastly, the passage in 1 Thessalonians raises the matter of *capability*. Can anyone really live by these high standards in a sex-saturated society? Isn't it taken for granted a person will have an active sex life regardless of whether he is married?

The answer to this lies in verse 8 where God offers His resources. "God . . . bestows on you his Holy Spirit" (1 Thessalonians 4:8, *NEB*). This means He provides the strength to resist temptation and keep sex under control. God doesn't ask us to do this on our own. He doesn't ask us to reach an unattainable goal. He has promised His help, dynamic power, care and protection. When a Christian yields himself totally to Christ (including his sex life) he experiences the amazing truth of Philippians 2:13 (*TLB*): "God is at work within you, helping you want to obey him, and then helping you do what he wants."

The second passage you may want to call to the attention of your children is 1 Corinthians 6:12-20. Read it in several translations. You will notice it has much the same emphasis as 1 Thessalonians. The Christian is told in verse 18 to "flee fornication," or as J. B. Phillips paraphrases it: "Avoid sexual looseness like the plague." *The Living Bible* says, "Run from sex sin." An excellent illustration of this principle is the story of youthful Joseph fleeing from Potiphar's wife after her attempted seduction (Genesis 39—note especially verses 9 and 12).

First Corinthians 6 answers those who say sex is a physical appetite and should be indulged like any other. If a person is thirsty, he gets a drink. If he's hungry, he looks for food. If he's sleepy, he can take a nap. Why can't sex be thought of in the same way? The Corinthians tried this reasoning with Paul. "Food is meant for the stomach and the stomach for food," said the Corinthians. Just wait a minute, said Paul. It's not that simple. Food, and the stomach have to do with physical, temporal matters. Sex is different. It's more than physical because the body is meant for the Lord. To misuse your bodies sexually is to misuse parts of *His* body! Can you imagine parts of Christ's body being linked and made one flesh with temple prostitutes? Never, never, never. In addition, your body has *eternal* significance and will be raised like Christ's body; it must not be sinned against by sexual abuse. Your body is the temple of the Holy Spirit. And what is more, your body doesn't even belong to you. It belongs to God because He purchased it with the great price of Christ's own blood. You are not your own!

This is the thrust of Paul's words to the Christians who lived in the midst of a society known as one of the most flagrantly immoral, sexually loose places on earth. Many of the Christians indulged in fornication, adultery, and homosexual acts before their conversion. Now things had changed. But still they, as we do, faced temptations. Paul's counsel can be helpful to modern Christians just as it was in the first century.

Let's look at a brief passage in the Gospels—some words of Jesus about marriage. He bases his remarks on Genesis 1:27 and 2:24.

"Have you not read that he who made them from the beginning made them male and female, and said, 'For this reason a man shall leave his father and mother and be joined to his wife, and the two shall become one'? So they are no longer two but one (flesh). What therefore God has joined together, let no man put asunder" (Matthew 19:4-6).

We notice here the sequence, leave—cleave—become one flesh.[11] This is mentioned for a specific purpose. In the passages that warned against fornication, a doubt was left in the minds of some new morality supporters. They said these warnings were speaking only of casual, promiscuous sexual relations with prostitutes. They say the Bible does not clearly forbid sex relations for couples who are engaged, in love, or in some way deeply committed to each other.

But Jesus pointed out that God created male and female to be united in a relationship that involved a lifelong commitment. There would be three main aspects to the relationship. First, a public declaration, a socially recognized, legitimate change in status from "single" to "married." "Therefore a man shall leave his father and mother." There is a movement away from one family in order to enter another. The second part, "a man shall cleave or be joined to his wife." A new social unit is formed; the foundation of a new family is laid down. And the third part; the couple now has the privilege of becoming one flesh, in the fullest sense of the word.

The Bible makes clear these three parts of marriage

84

belong together, and the sequence of events must be observed.

Let's Talk It Over

1. Do you agree with the statement that parents seem to find it more difficult to teach the moral side of sex than to teach about the physical facts? Discuss.

2. Discuss the three areas that parents must keep in mind in guiding their children in sex ethics. Why is *each* important?

3. Clip from magazines, newspapers and advice columns, articles reflecting confusion about prevalent sex standards. How do these clippings illustate points made in this chapter?

4. Why are the old arguments for premarital chastity not convincing to many young people today?

5. How can we help our children accept *as their own* a workable, meaningful, Christian sex ethic for the times in which we live? What is the difference between a moral standard that is centered in rules and one that is centered in Christ?

6. Would you agree that it was just as difficult during Old and New Testament times to teach God's sex standards as it is today? Why or why not?

7. *When* should a child begin learning Christian moral standards?

8. What do the three main Bible passages cited (1 Thessalonians 4; 1 Corinthians 6; Matthew 19) have to say to modern young people in the midst of today's questioning about sex standards? What do you feel is the most important teaching in these passages? Why?

References

1. "Dear Abby," *Bloomington Herald-Telephone*, Bloomington, Indiana, Oct. 24, 1968.

2. Ira Reiss, "Sexual Relationships in the 1970's," Lec-

ture given at Indiana University, Bloomington, Ind., April 23, 1970.

3. Ira L. Reiss, *Premarital Sexual Standards in America* (New York: The Free Press, 1960).

4. Ira L. Reiss, 1970 lecture at Indiana University.

5. Alfred C. Kinsey, Wardell B. Pomeroy, and Clyde E. Martin, *Sexual Behavior in the Human Male* (Philadelphia: W. B. Saunders Co., 1948). More recent studies by Indiana University's Institute for Sex Research, founded by the late Dr. Kinsey, indicate similar findings, as do other studies.

6. The 1971 Kantner and Zelnik study, recognized by sociologists as *the* definitive work in the area of premarital sexual behavior research up until this point in time, shows some changes in the sexual conduct of girls—though they are not so extensive and dramatic as sensational news reports have led many to believe. Professors John F. Kantner and Melvin Zelnik of Johns Hopkins University, working under a research grant from the National Institute of Child Health and Human Development, Department of Health, Education and Welfare, obtained data from interviews of a national random representative sample of 4,240 never-married young women, ages 15-19. Included in the survey were both blacks and whites and girls of both higher and lower socioeconomic status, and these factors accounted for differences in sexual experience. But taken all together, it was found that 27.6 percent of 15- to 19-year-old girls have had premarital sexual intercourse (or roughly, three out of every ten girls). The likelihood of a girl's having intercourse increases with each year of age—for example, 13.8 percent of the 15-year-olds had engaged in premarital sex, compared to 46.1 percent of the 19-year-olds. Furthermore, Kantner and Zelnik see a pattern which indicates that more girls will become sexually experienced at an earlier

age. They write: "Our conservative estimate is that a minimum of three percent of those 19 in 1971 were likely to have had sexual intercourse by age 15, compared to nine percent of those who were currently 15" (p. 10). But apart from shifts of this sort, there does not appear to be the dramatic upsurge in promiscuity that may seem evident to the casual observer. In fact, three-fifths of the sexually experienced girls in the survey had only had one partner ever, and half of them had had intercourse only with their future husband. (This is interesting in view of the Kinsey studies twenty years earlier which showed that approximately 50 percent of women entered marriage nonvirginal, and of these nearly half had confined their sexual experience to relations with the man they would marry.) See John F. Kantner and Melvin Zelnik, "Sexual Experience of Young Unmarried Women in the United States," *Family Planning Perspectives,* Vol. 4, No. 4 (October, 1972), pp. 9-18.

7. It may be significant that in a 1967 survey of college students from schools across the nation, it was found that fourteen percent of males reported that their first sexual intercourse had taken place with girls they intended to marry. This was true of less than five percent in surveys during the 1940's. During the forties, nearly one-fourth of males reported that their first experience of intercourse occurred with a prostitute. By 1967, such was the case with only from two to seven percent. These statistics, reported in surveys conducted by Indiana University's Institute for Sex Research, were cited in Alton Blakeslee, "There's No Sexual Revolution" (AP report), *The Bloomington Herald-Telephone,* Bloomington, Indiana, December 29, 1967.

8. William A. Daniel, Jr., *The Adolescent Patient* (Saint Louis: The C. V. Mosby Company, 1970), p. 78.

9. Mary Douglas, *Purity and Danger—An Analysis of Concepts of Pollution and Taboo* (Harmondsworth,

Middlesex, England: Penguin Books Ltd., Pelican Books edition, 1970), p. 179.

10. Walter Goodman, "The New Sex Education," *Redbook*, Vol. 129, No. 5 (Sept. 1967), p. 140.

11. This point is discussed in considerable detail in my book, *Sex and the Single Eye* (Grand Rapids, Mich.: Zondervan Publishing House, 1968), pp. 92-98,115. The point is also made in Walter Trobisch's excellent book, *I Married You* (New York: Harper & Row Publishers, 1971); see especially chapter two.

CHAPTER FIVE

The Female Body: God's Design

"You created every part of me," said the Psalmist. "You put me together in my mother's womb" (Psalm 139:13, *TEV*). Yet most of us seem afraid and embarrassed about our bodies' natural functions. We are especially ill at ease about the parts of our body connected with sex. Even after marriage and childbirth, sex organs and sexual processes remain a mystery to many adults. Is it because of a sense of shame? If so, it's almost as though we don't really believe God created the sex organs! (See "Nudity," chapter 8.)

Most people, whether or not they admit it, are curious about sex. That's why books about sex often find their way to the best-seller lists. And we should know about our sexuality because every part of the human body is a work of God. To learn about His works is to learn about the power and wisdom of God. It's in this spirit the Christian should find out about sex and reproduction. "Great are the works of the Lord, studied by all who have pleasure in them" (Psalm 111:2). With this attitude as our guide, let's look at God's design for the female body.

Sex Characteristics

God designed the bodies of human males and females to be different from one another. Some differences are obvious from birth; others develop at puberty. Differences of the first type are called *primary* sex characteristics and refer to basic reproductive equipment. Thus, a doctor who has just delivered a baby tells a mother, "It's a boy!" because he has observed the tiny penis and the scrotum between the infant's legs. If the physician sees two folds of skin that enclose a tiny clitoris and vaginal and urinary openings, he tells the mother, "It's a girl!" These are the *external* signs of femaleness. Inside her body are the most essential primary structures that make reproduction possible.

The Creator also planned the bodies of men and women to differ in ways other than primary sex characteristics. Not only are the genital organs different; males and females are physically distinctive.

These distinctions are called *secondary* sex characteristics. Secondary sex characteristics in girls occur at the beginning of puberty and include the development of breasts, onset of menstruation, rounding out of the hips, and a new distribution of body fat causing a softer, shapelier, womanly appearance. As these changes occur, hair begins to grow under the arms and in the pubic region. A girl's voice also matures, becoming slightly fuller and deeper as the larynx enlarges. She begins to speak in the tones of a woman, for that is what she is becoming.

The word "puberty" comes from Latin words meaning, "grown-up," "adulthood," "groin," and "body hair." Puberty is the time when the body becomes capable of reproduction. For girls, this is usually signaled by the beginning of menstruation. The average beginning age for menstruation is about twelve. But many girls have their first period earlier (sometimes as early as age nine), and others don't begin until as late as sixteen or seventeen.

90

Such variations are normal and are not cause for alarm.

You may have heard of a period of "adolescent sterility" in young girls. This means that some female bodies do not release ova with any regularity until several months or even years after the first menstrual period. During this time, conception would not likely occur. But one cannot be certain about the *exact* time when a girl is able to have a baby—as may be seen in the occasional tragic reports of pregnant eleven and twelve-year-olds. Menstruation for some girls *does* mean they have become capable of reproduction. In fact, there are even cases in which young girls have become pregnant before menstrual periods have begun![1]

What is it that changes a girl's body from child to woman? How does the body "know" the time for puberty has arrived? The answer is a matter of glands and chemistry. When you hear the word "gland," you probably think of sweat, tear, or salivary glands and the secretions they pour out from their ducts to do special jobs like cooling the skin, cleansing the eyes, or moistening food. There are other kinds of glands, however, that do other jobs. They're called *endocrine glands* or "glands of internal secretion." They don't have ducts or channels to discharge their secretions. Instead they produce special chemical products that are absorbed by the blood vessels. These chemical substances are called *hormones*. Their task is to serve as messengers. Carried by the bloodstream, they travel through the body to produce specific effects on various organs, tissues, and other glands.

The *gonads*, or sex glands, belong to the endocrine system. They produce "messengers" that act on various parts of the body to produce the changes associated with puberty. The female gonads are the *ovaries*, and they secrete hormones (estrogen and progesterone) which have special parts to play in the development of a girl's secondary sex characteristics. These hormones also control

91

the functioning of the menstrual cycle, and the complex processes associated with pregnancy and the production of milk for the newborn baby.

How do the gonads know when to send their messengers to the organs they influence? The *pituitary gland,* located below the brain and deep within the head (near its center), sometimes called the "master control," sends the signals. One of the tasks of this tiny, pea-size gland is to send hormone messengers to the ovaries so they will mature and begin to produce other hormones. These hormones gradually transform a little girl into a woman.

If the sex glands are the producers of hormones that trigger important changes at puberty, what keeps them from producing these hormones earlier in life? It has to do with God's marvelous design of the pituitary gland. Before a baby is born, the sex glands do produce internal secretions which help differentiate the sex organs of males and females. But from the time a child is born up until he reaches puberty, the gonads are held in check by *another* hormone produced by the pituitary gland.[2] Everything is timed and designed to happen the way God planned.

Sex Structures on the Outside of a Woman's Body

Due to their body structure, boys are usually more familiar with their sex organs than girls. Even grown women often regard their sexual systems as great mysteries and have only the foggiest notion of how they work. To understand the female body, it may help to become acquainted with the women's outside structure.

The Breasts

The two dome-shaped protrusions from a woman's chest are some of the most obvious signs of femaleness. These organs are *erogenous zones* and are sensitive to

92

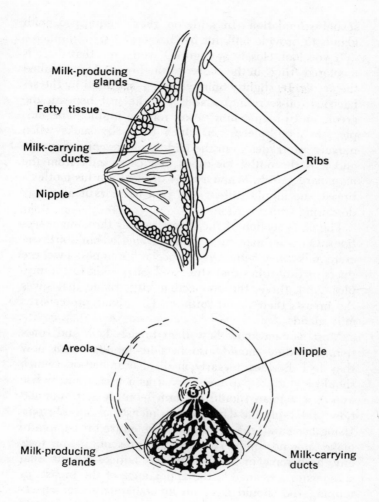

Figure 1 Female Breast

sexual stimulation. In addition they're equipped with glands to provide milk for her baby.

If you look closely at Figure 1, you'll not that there is a colored "ring" in the center of the breast. This is called the *areola*. Its slightly bumpy surface is caused by the sebaceous (oil-secreting) glands that lie just beneath the areola and provide lubrication for the nipple. The nipple, or "mouthpiece" on which the baby sucks when nursing, protrudes from the middle of the colored areola and it is the outlet for tubes that carry milk from the *mammary glands*. When a baby drinks from his mother's breast, the nipple stiffens and protrudes, as it also may do during sexual excitement.[3]

The cross section of the breast reveals three main sections. One, the mammary glands which at childbirth secrete milk when activated by special hormones. Two, the ducts or tiny tubes that store and carry milk to the nipples. And, three, the connecting fatty tissue that gives the breasts their round softness. This tissue protects the milk glands.

Most women know how their breasts look and function. But they should also become familiar with how they feel. Besides a yearly medical examination (which should include a pap test as well as a breast and pelvic exam), a woman should perform monthly self-examination, preferably the day after her menstrual period stops. Using her hand, she can go over the entire breast area to make sure no lumps (tumors) are present. If she feels any hardening or thickening, or notices an unusual soreness or a change in the appearance of the breasts or nipples, she should have an immediate medical checkup. Not all breast tumors are cancerous, but it's best to be certain. Also, unusual discharges from the nipples should be reported to a physician.

As puberty approaches, breast development takes place because of the triggering of estrogen hormones.

The breasts may feel tender and full at this time which is nothing to worry about. It also is normal for some girls to have a small secretion from the nipples.[4] During this time of breast development, many girls need parental understanding and reassurance. Many girls worry about their breasts filling out too much, or not enough. They feel embarrassment about their changing appearance. And some are unenthused about becoming a woman. During these growing stages, parents can help give their daughters self-esteem and positive acceptance of God's beautiful design for their bodies.

The Vulva

The second outside sex structure of a woman's body is the *vulva* area. Sometimes this part of the body is spoken of as the external female genitalia, or simply as "the genitals." Figure 2 shows how this part of the body would appear to a woman if she held a mirror between her legs. (Incidentally, if this shocks or suggests something "dirty," you might want to reexamine your attitudes toward the human body. If you honestly believe it's a beautifully designed creation of God, you won't feel shameful.)

On the front, lower part of a woman's body, the triangular patch of pubic hair covers a mound of fatty tissue called the *mons veneris*. Translated, it means "the mountain of Venus," and was named for the ancient Roman goddess of love. Underneath this layer of fatty tissue is the pubic bone.

Between a woman's legs are two pairs of "lips" or *labia*, one pair enfolding the other. The outer lips (*labia majora* or larger lips) are made up of fatty tissue and are covered with hair. They are much thicker than the inner lips (the *labia minora* or smaller lips), which are thinner folds of skin covered with mucous membrane.

Notice the location of the *clitoris*. This is the most sexually sensitive structure in a woman's body and plays an

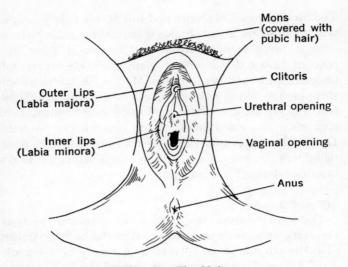

**Figure 2   The Vulva
(external female genitalia)**

important part in making sexual intercourse a wonderful, pleasurable experience. It is richly supplied with nerves and blood vessels, and like the male penis, becomes engorged with blood during sexual excitement. The clitoris is sometimes compared to a male's penis because it has a very sensitive "head" (glans) and is covered by a soft fold of skin like the uncircumcised penis and slightly increases in size during foreplay. However, it has no urinary opening as does the penis nor does the clitoris play a part in the reproductive process. It is solely an organ for sexual arousal and pleasure.

Notice also the women's body has three openings, each with a special purpose. It's important to keep this in mind when answering children's questions about reproduction. Make sure children understand that God made a special passageway through which babies enter the world. They don't come out of the opening through which urine passes (*urethral opening*), nor from the opening through which solid wastes pass from the intestines (anus). Babies enter the world through the *vagina*.

Vagina is the Latin word for "sheath," and suggests the close-fitting case in which a soldier placed his sword. The vagina then is the "tube" in which a man places his penis during sexual intercourse. The opening to the vagina is shown in Figure 2.

To facilitate sexual intercourse, God has equipped the female body with special lubricating glands. The most important of these are the Bartholin glands, located on each side of the vagina near its outside opening.

Across the opening of the vagina, stretches a thin membrane called the *hymen* or "maidenhead." The act of breaking through the hymen during the first intercourse is sometimes called "defloration." In many ways, this is an unfortunate term, because it literally means "a plucking of flowers," a stripping away of something beautiful, or a despoiling of something fresh and whole. It has the thought of ravishing and taking away a woman's virginity, rather than emphasizing the positive view that marriage is a giving to each other, not stealing something.

In many ancient cultures and in parts of the world today the unbroken hymen is considered the symbol of virginity. And in some ancient cultures newlyweds displayed blood-stained sheets after their first intercourse as proof of virginity. This explains the "tokens of virginity" mentioned in Deuteronomy 22:13-21.

The hymen, unfortunately, has been emphasized out of proportion to its actual significance. Its biological purpose is to protect girls from infection during early childhood by keeping out certain microorganisms which, after puberty, are warded off by the secretions of the vagina.[5] Furthermore, an intact hymen is not necessarily "proof" of premarital abstinence. Some women have had considerable sexual intimacies without penetration by a penis. Some women have hymens which stretch and are not ruptured at intercourse. Conversely, a woman may be a virgin, but her hymen may have been torn before marriage by some means completely unrelated to sex. Vigorous exercise, for example, or forcing a tampon through an extremely small opening. The absence of a hymen in such a woman certainly doesn't mean loss of virginity!

The hymen is not totally closed. It has one or more perforations through which the menstrual fluid can pass. In some women the opening is very small; in others, it may be so large that the hymen itself seems to be only a thin ring of tissue surrounding the vaginal opening. There is also great variation in the thickness of the hymen.

Sex Structures on the Inside of a Woman's Body

In contrast to the way God has designed the male body, the major reproductive organs of a woman lie within her body and are not observable. Because of this, women need to become acquainted with these basic internal structures.

The Uterus

The uterus (sometimes called the "womb") is the organ in which the unborn child develops. Located in the pelvic area, it's about the size and shape of a pear. Think of this "pear" as having its stem end downward. The stem is also slightly tilted toward the rear of the body. (See Figure 4.)

The muscular walls are amazing in their capacity to expand. The uterus of a non-pregnant woman is only about three inches long and two inches wide; yet upon conception, it begins to enlarge until it holds a fully developed infant who may weigh eight or nine pounds and be twenty inches long!

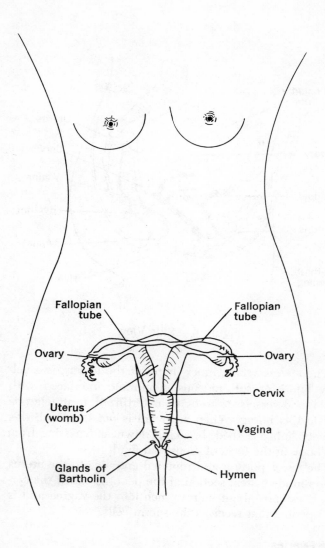

Figure 3   Front View

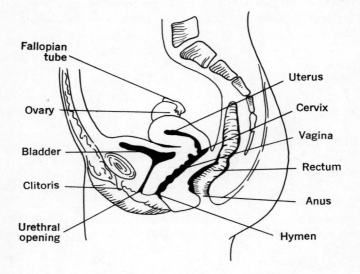

Figure 4   Side View

The *endometrium,* inner lining of the uterus, is a velvety lining of soft mucous membrane interlaced with tiny blood vessels. If an ovum is fertilized, it attaches itself to this lining. When an ovum is *not* fertilized, this velvety lining is shed, breaking down and passing from the body in the form of menstrual fluid.

The lower portion and rounded entrance to the uterus (the rounded, stem section of the pear) is called the *cervix.* It extends about half an inch into the vagina and is the opening that receives the sperm cells.

The Ovaries

As mentioned earlier, the ovaries are the female *gonads* or sex glands that have an important hormone-producing function. In addition, they have a reproductive function, by holding and releasing the egg cells (*ova*). Conception and pregnancy take place when an ovum and male sperm cell are joined.

The woman's body has one small oval shaped ovary on either side of the uterus. (See Figure 3.) They are small (about 2 x 1 inches in diameter), yet contain thousands of egg cells. Once a month in a process called ovulation, an egg is released from one of the ovaries.

The Fallopian Tubes

Partially encircling the ovaries are tubes with "fringes," or fingerlike projections, around their open ends. They are not attached to the ovaries, but are close to them so that they can receive released eggs and conduct them toward the uterus. Sometimes called "oviducts" or "uterine tubes," these important parts of the female reproductive system are most familiarly known as the *Fallopian tubes* (their name coming from an Italian anatomist, Fallopius, who first described them). It is in the Fallopian tubes that the egg and sperm must meet if conception is to take place.

If you like to use your imagination, think of the journey of an ovum from the ovary, through the tube, and (if not fertilized) through the uterus and out of the body. Pretend you are standing with both arms outstretched from your body (toward the left and toward the right) and slightly raised. In each hand is a small bag of marbles. From one of the bags, a tiny marble squeezes out and slowly begins to roll down the sleeve of your sweater, then down through your chest, and eventually out of your clothing and onto the floor. This gives you a crude idea of the process. The marble bags represent the ovaries, the marble the released ovum, the hands the fingerlike projections that seem to guide the released ovum into the Fallopian tubes, and the sweater sleeve il-

101

lustrates the Fallopian tubes leading into the uterus. (Study Figure 3.)

The Vagina

The vagina is the tubular cavity into which the penis is inserted or thrust during copulation. It is about three to four inches long, but being made up of muscle and tissue, it is very elastic and is capable of great stretching. It has an inner lining of mucous membrane and becomes liberally lubricated during sexual arousal. Ordinarily, the walls of the vagina touch each other, much like a child's balloon before it is inflated. When they receive a penis, a tampon, or through childbirth, they separate. Since the vagina is the passageway through which a baby is born, it is sometimes called the birth canal. The vagina is also, of course, the channel through which the menstrual flow passes.

God's design of the female body is something we can't help but ponder with amazement and awe. But our sense of wonder will be just as great as we look at God's other masterpiece, the male body.

Let's Talk It Over

1. Do you agree with the statement that many adults are unfamiliar with the design and workings of the sexual structures that are part of their own bodies? Give reasons for your opinion on this and any examples you can think of.

2. Why is it that some girls, as they approach puberty, seem to find it difficult to accept their budding womanhood? How can we as Christian parents help them to have a positive outlook on the changes that are taking place in their bodies?

3. Look back over the drawings in this chapter. Do you clearly understand these parts of the body and how they function? Can you name the various parts? How

would you use these pictures in explaining to an older child or teen-ager God's design for the female body?

4. The writer of Psalm 139 praised God for His marvelous work in creating the human body and expressed great joy and wonder at the processes connected with reproduction. The growth of a child in the uterus was a cause for worshiping God. With this in mind, and thinking back over the contents of this chapter you have just read on God's design for the female body, compose your own psalm of praise for what God has made. Or write a prayer thanking God for the gift of sex and for the beauty and functioning of the female body.

References

1. See the section on adolescent development in *Sexuality and Man*, compiled and edited by the Sex Information and Education Council of the United States (New York: Charles Scribner's Sons, 1970), p. 28. See also Eric W. Johnson, *Sex: Telling It Straight* (Philadelphia: J. B. Lippincott Co., 1970), p. 23.

2. This is the growth-stimulating hormone. See C. E. Turner, *Personal and Community Health* (St. Louis: The C. V. Mosby Co., 1967 edition), pp. 48-49.

3. Lawrence Crawley, James Malfetti, Ernest Stewart, and Nina Vas Dias, *Reproduction, Sex and Preparation for Marriage* (Englewood Cliffs, N. J.: Prentice-Hall, Inc., 1964), p. 33.

4. *The Life Cycle Library for Young People*, Vol. 1 (Chicago: The Parent and Child Institute, 1969), p. 57.

5. Crawley, et al., *Reproduction, Sex and Preparation for Marriage*, p. 29.

CHAPTER SIX

The Male Body: God's Design

As with women, men have both primary and secondary sex characteristics. The *primary* sex characteristics are body parts essential to the male's role in reproduction. No doubt the penis and testicles are the first structures you think of when referring to basic differences between men and women.

But there are also *secondary* sex characteristics that occur with the onset of puberty; the growth of hair under the arms and in the genital area, facial hair and thickening of hair on the arms, legs and chest. There is a thickening of muscle fibers which give the male body its particular muscular physique. The voice deepens and as the voice box enlarges, it usually drops a full octave.[1] (You can help young children understand an older brother's voice change by explaining that high-pitched tones on a harp come from the short strings at the top and low-pitched tones from the longer strings. Because men have bigger vocal cords than women, their voices are deeper. Plucking a thick and thin rubber band also illustrates the difference.)

As these changes take place, the penis and scrotum enlarge and the pubic hair becomes more plentiful, darker, coarser, and somewhat curly. In some men, there is a line of hair extending from the pubic area up to the navel. Children sometimes wonder if a person's pubic hair is the same color as the hair on his head; the answer is, "usually, yes."

As with girls, boys' secondary characteristics occur because of hormones. The male hormones are called *androgens*. Of importance is a hormone produced in the testicles called *testosterone*. This is the hormone that the pituitary gland "commands" the testicles to begin producing when a boy approaches puberty. The testosterone then gets busy to change a boy into a man. There is also growth and development in the primary sex characteristics. The testicles begin producing reproductive cells called sperm cells. When a boy first ejaculates sperm cells from his body through the penis, he is said to have reached puberty. Biologically, he is now capable of becoming a father. There is, however, a great deal of variation between the time boys reach puberty. Some may be as young as ten, others sixteen or seventeen. There is no reason to worry if a boy seems to be developing slowly or more rapidly than other boys his age.

The testicles also manufacture a small amount of the female hormone (estrogen). And a woman's body also produces male hormones (androgens). But in a man, there is more testosterone than there is estrogen, while the opposite is the case with women.[2] Many people are surprised to learn that our bodies contain *both* male and female hormones.

Male Sex Organs—the Outside

In understanding God's design for the male body, we first notice that unlike the female body, the organs of reproduction lie on the outside. The first reason for this has

to do with the physical act of being made "one flesh."
The male penis was planned in such a way that it can fit
inside a woman's vagina. The second reason for *external*
male genitals relates to temperature. Heat reduces
sperm-producing capacity—even internal body heat.
That's why, in the plan of God, the testicles were placed
in a special bag outside the body. There, they are kept at
a temperature about one degree lower than normal body
temperature.[3]

The Penis

Hanging from the lower pelvic area, the cylindrical
penis lies limply against the sac which holds the testicles.
The cone-shaped head of the penis is called the *glans*
and is richly supplied with nerve endings which make it
extremely sensitive to sexual stimulation. Like the glans
of a woman's clitoris, it is a primary focus of sensual
pleasure, more so than any other area of the body.

The second main part of the penis is the *shaft* or body.
It is covered with loose, retractable skin, which at birth
not only covers the shaft in sheathlike fashion, but also
extends over the glans. This extended covering is called
the *foreskin* or *prepuce*. It is often surgically removed a
few days after birth to make it easier to keep the penis
clean.

When a man becomes sexually excited, blood flows
into the spongy tissues that make up the penis until they
become engorged. Veins leading away from the penis are
temporarily constricted at this time, causing the cavern-
ous tissue of the penis to remain blood-filled, with the
result that the size of the penis is greatly enlarged.[4] This
is called an *erection* and is essential for sexual intercourse. Without an erection, a man cannot insert his
penis into the vagina of a woman.

Penises vary greatly in size, as do other parts of the
human body, and this variation among men is nothing to

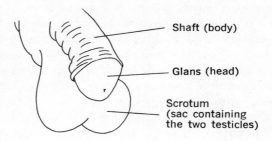

**Figure 5   The Penis
(circumcised)**

worry about. The size of a man's penis does *not* determine the amount of sexual pleasure he is able to receive for himself or provide for his wife. During erection, penises are more similar in size than in the flaccid state. Smaller penises tend to have a greater relative size increase than do larger ones. In its relaxed state, the average size of a penis is about three inches long. In an erection, its length increases to an average of six inches, with a slight increase in diameter.[5]

In an erection, the penis is not only enlarged, it is also stiff and hard. It projects outward and upward from the body at an angle. Sexual stimulation, whether from actual sexual activity, from thoughts about sex, reading erotic literature, or pictures, is likely to result in an erection. But boys and men have erections for other reasons. It isn't unusual to see erect penises in even the tiniest babies. A full bladder, straining during bowel movements, exposure to cold, tight clothing, washing the genitals, and dreaming are some reasons for erections. Boys should understand this to be a normal part of being a male. Dr. Wardell Pomeroy points out that teen-age boys worry about erections occurring in public. He suggests directing one's thoughts away from sexual matters helps bring the penis back to its flaccid state.[6]

Inside the penis is a tube called the *urethra*. Its opening is at the tip of the glans. The urethra carries urine from the bladder to be eliminated, and in ejaculation, carries the sperm cells. God designed the body so that the two functions are kept separate. (Sometimes children, when first learning about intercourse, wonder if urine from the husband will pass into the wife. The answer is no; a system of valves prevents this from happening.)

The Scrotum

A small sac or pouch called the *scrotum* hangs below the penis to hold the two testicles. Correct temperature is important for sperm to be produced and the scrotum is designed to keep the testicles at just the right level of warmth. Boys may notice when their bodies become chilled, the scrotum draws up close to the body to keep the testicles warmer. But when taking a hot shower, the pouch hangs very loose. In this way, the testicles are kept farther away from the body and therefore cooler. Again, this "thermostatic control system" is an amazing indication of the Creator's magnificent design.

To protect this area from injury during vigorous sports activities, boys often wear an athletic supporter called a jockstrap.

The Breasts

The male has two small colored nipples on each side of his chest. But the breasts of men do not develop into milk-producing organs like those of women. Instead, their function seems to be like other erogenous body zones, to provide sexual pleasure, something wives should keep in mind. (The body's erogenous zones are

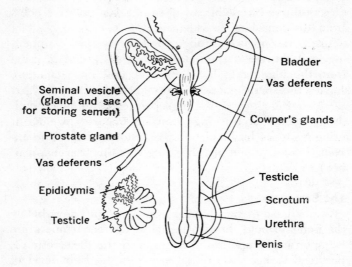

Figure 6   Front View

especially supplied with nerve endings and are extremely sensitive to sexual stimulation.)

At the approach of puberty, boys often notice their breasts becoming tender, sensitive, and slightly puffed. This is normal and is part of the tremendous change occurring through increased activities of the endocrine glands and their hormones as the body of a boy changes to that of a man.

Male Sex Organs—the Inside

The Testicles

The testicles or *testes* (either term is acceptable) may be compared to the ovaries in the female and also have a similar twofold function. First, the testes are male gonads, sex glands which produce important male hormones.

110

Second, they serve as factories for the production of sperm cells or *spermatozoa*. These are the male cells designed to join with the female cells (the eggs or ova) in order for reproduction to take place.

There are two testicles, one of which hangs slightly lower than the other within the scrotum. They are oval-shaped and contain hundreds of tiny tubes where the sperm cells are manufactured. Sperm-production starts at puberty and continues throughout a man's lifetime. At one time, it was thought men were provided with a certain supply of sperm cells when they were born and that this supply must be guarded carefully so that it did not become depleted. These fears are groundless. Healthy male bodies constantly produce *millions* of sperm cells.

The Epididymis

Over the top and back of each testicle is a special place for storing sperm cells. God designed this unusual organ as a place to ripen these cells and eliminate faulty sperm. These maturation chambers are called the epididymides and may be seen on Figure 6.

Each epididymis is about two inches long, but is made up of an extremely tiny tube coiled up like a ball of string which if stretched out would measure about twenty feet long!'

The Vas Deferens

As sperm cells continue their journey from the testicles, they leave the epididymis and move up through the vas deferens, a tube about seventeen inches long. There are two of these sperm-carrying tubes, one leading from each testicle.

In their journey through the vas deferens, the sperm cells do not move under their own power but are moved along by muscle contractions and tiny cilia (hairlike structures in the lining of the tube).

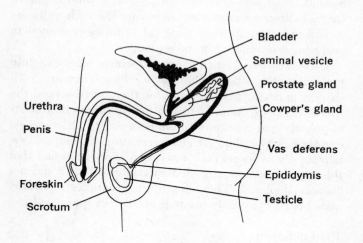

Figure 7   Side View

The Seminal Vesicles

Before the sperm cells reach the urethra, they pass through an area where the vas deferens is met by a tiny canal which leads from a small "bag" called a seminal vesicle. One of these is located on each side, just as there are two testicles, two epididymes, and two vasa deferentia (tubes). What happens at this juncture in the journey? Some sperm cells are stored in this area. In addition, a secretion from the seminal vesicle gland acts on the sperm cells enabling them to move freely on their own power.

The Prostate Gland

The prostate gland is located under the bladder and near the seminal vesicles. The secretion of the prostate gland, like that of the seminal vesicles, joins with the sperm cells and makes up the sticky fluid called *semen*.

It aids the sperm cells in their ability to move. Because it is alkaline, the secretion helps to counteract the acid condition of a woman's vagina that would otherwise kill the sperm cells.[8]

Sometimes the prostate gland becomes infected, enlarged, or diseased. If it is surgically removed, it is still possible for men to be sexually active and sire children.

Cowper's Glands

The urethra of a male, like a woman's vagina, must have its acidity neutralized if sperm cells are to live. Two tiny glands, called Cowper's glands, take care of this problem. When a man is sexually stimulated the Cowper's glands provide an alkaline fluid which passes through the urethra. This prepares the urethra for the passage of the sperm cells by neutralizing the acid and providing lubrication.[9] Before ejaculation, an overflow of this secretion may ooze from the tip of the penis. Sometimes a small number of sperm cells are present in this secretion. For this reason the "withdrawal" method of birth control is risky. A penis in a vagina before ejaculation can discharge sperm cells and possibly cause a pregnancy.

Ejaculation

The word *ejaculate* comes from a Latin term meaning to shoot out, to hurl, or throw out. It accurately describes the way the sperm cells leave the body when a man reaches the point of sexual climax or *orgasm*. At the height of sexual excitement, muscles in the genital area contract and the semen jets out in a series of quick spurts. It seems like the body is undergoing a momentary spasm.

At the peak of sexual arousal, many things happen at once. Ducts open up to let out sperm cells from their storage places. Secretions from the seminal vesicles and prostate gland rush to mix with sperm cells. Muscles of

113

the penis contract to propel the semen so that it is forced through the urethra.

Ejaculation may occur through sexual intercourse, through masturbation, or through a *nocturnal emission* (sometimes called a "wet dream"). Nocturnal emissions are normal occurrences in boys after puberty. During sleep, while dreaming, a boy may have an orgasm and awake to find there has been an ejaculation of semen. There is no reason to feel ashamed or guilty. This is a perfectly normal part of sexual development. Some writers suggest these dreams occur as a natural, automatic method for the release of excess semen.[10] Others say they result from sexual tensions and sexual dreams and do not necessarily take place after a long period of sexual abstinence and a buildup of semen. They may occur even in the sleep of a young man who has had intercourse the same night.[11] No doubt there is truth in both explanations. Christian boys may be helped to realize that, although we are responsible for the control of our *conscious* thoughts, dreams are not something we can control. They needn't cause guilt.

Let's Talk It Over

1. Make a list of similarities and differences in the male and female reproductive systems. (Think, for example, of the twofold function of the gonads in each sex.)

2. Using the diagrams, try to describe in simple terms what happens from the time sperm cells are produced until they are ejaculated from the penis. This exercise is not only an aid to your own understanding, but is good practice for the time when you must explain the process to your children.

3. What are some *specific* evidences of God's wisdom in His design of the male reproductive system? Make a list.

114

4. Compose a prayer of thanksgiving in which you give praise to God for the wonderful workings of the male body.

References

1. William A. Daniel, Jr., *The Adolesccent Patient* (Saint Louis: C. V. Mosby Co., 1970), p. 361.

2. Lawrence Q. Crawley, James L. Malfetti, Ernest I. Stewart, and Nina Vas Dias, *Reproduction, Sex, and Preparation for Marriage* (Englewood Cliffs, N.J.: Prentice-Hall, Inc., 1964), p. 9.

3. Crawley, et al., p. 4.

4. Justus J. Schifferes, *Family Medical Encyclopedia* (New York: Pocket Books, Inc., Permabook edition, 1959), p. 473.

5. Crawley, et al., p. 12.

6. Wardell B. Pomeroy, *Boys and Sex* (New York: Dell Publishing Co. paper back edition, 1968), p. 149.

7. Crawley, et al., p. 8; Schifferes' *Family Medical Encyclopedia,* p. 470.

8. Crawley, et al., p. 11.

9. Crawley, et al., p. 13.

10. See Schifferes' *Family Medical Encyclopedia,* p. 472; Paul Bohannan, *Love, Sex and Being Human* (Garden City, N. Y.: Doubleday and Company, Inc., 1970), p. 41; A. J. Bueltmann, *Take the High Road* (Saint Louis: Concordia Publishing House, 1967), p. 46; and Herbert J. Miles, *Sexual Understanding Before Marriage* (Grand Rapids: Zondervan Publishing House, 1971), p. 143; among others.

11. Crawley, et al., pp. 110-112; Pomeroy, pp. 148-49.

CHAPTER SEVEN

How Life Goes On

Have you ever tried to define *life?* It's not easy. One of the main characteristics of living things is that they can reproduce themselves. Living plants produce more living plants. Living animals give birth to other animals. And living humans give birth to other living human beings. Life goes on and on through the ever-repeating process of reproduction.

Everything connected with conception, pregnancy and birth is so natural and wonderful that it's hard to understand why we sometimes act ashamed and embarrassed about it! It is a tremendous, marvelous work of God! An accurate, reverent understanding of human reproduction is essential if parents are to carry out their responsibilities as sex educators.

In the two preceding chapters, human sex organs were described to give parents a basic understanding of body function and design. Now we want to build on that understanding and move to a discussion of how the sperm and egg cell meet, and how an infant grows in its mother's uterus.

As a further aid, the latter part of the chapter contains a description of the kinds of questions children are likely to ask about reproduction at various ages. Suggestions are also included to help you answer these and guide you in finding suitable teaching materials.

How Conception Takes Place

During sexual intercourse, the husband's erect penis is placed in the wife's vagina. At the time of sexual climax, semen is ejaculated from the penis. It spurts onto the mucus around the cervix (the neck or lower part of the uterus that extends slightly into the vagina). This mucus then "grabs" and holds onto the semen, attracting and stimulating the sperm cells[1] which next move through the opening of the cervix and up into the main body of the uterus. But the sperm cells don't stop there. They keep wriggling their tails, swimming up into the Fallo-

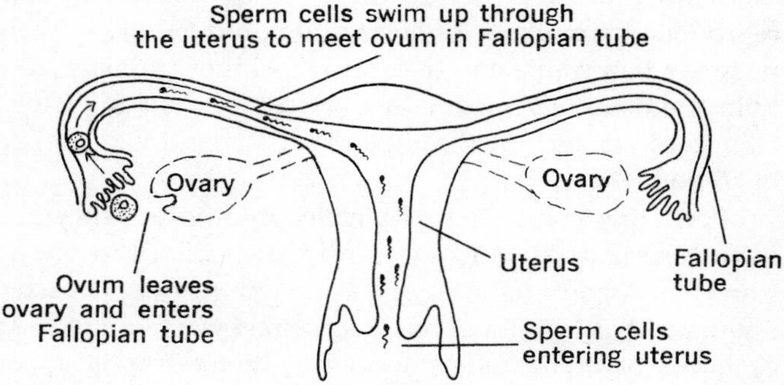

Sperm cells swim up through
the uterus to meet ovum in Fallopian tube

Ovary

Ovary

Ovum leaves
ovary and enters
Fallopian tube

Uterus

Fallopian
tube

Sperm cells
entering uterus

Figure 8
How Conception Takes Place (Part 1)

pian tubes. In one of these tubes, if it is the right time in the menstrual cycle, conception takes place. This means a ripe ovum (egg cell) must be in the tube so a sperm cell can join and fertilize it. This fertilized egg, now called a *zygote,* is the beginning of a pregnancy.

The fertilized ovum then continues traveling down the Fallopian tube (like the marble through the sweater sleeve). Only this time it stops in the uterus. It does not pass out of the body as do unfertilized ova, but rather burrows itself in the lining of the uterus. This mucous membrane lining has been building up since the last menstruation to act as a nesting place. It is richly supplied with blood and is designed to supply nourishment for the tiny cluster of beginning baby cells. Here, warm and snug, baby-to-be will develop for the next nine months. If fertilization of the ovum hasn't taken place, this thickened blood-filled special lining of the uterus breaks down once a month and passes out of the body as menstrual fluid.

The Amazing Egg and Sperm

When a baby girl is born, her tiny ovaries already contain thousands and thousands of immature, undeveloped egg cells.[2] Beginning at the time of puberty and continuing until menopause, some of these egg cells will be singled out for ripening. (Obviously, most of these thousands of egg follicles won't ever become ova, since the rate of ripening is only about one a month. This means the average woman would produce only about four or five hundred mature egg cells during her lifetime.[3] And even more obviously, only a very few of these hundreds of mature ova will ever be fertilized and develop into children.)

In the case of males, there is a continuous production of sperm cells from puberty onward. A man's body produces billions and billions of sperm during his lifetime. In fact, in just a single ejaculation of semen, there are usually 200 to 500 million sperm cells, sometimes even a billion![4] Yet, it takes just one sperm to start a baby. One of the main reasons for a high sperm count is to dissolve the hyaluronic acid that has cemented the ovum's layers

119

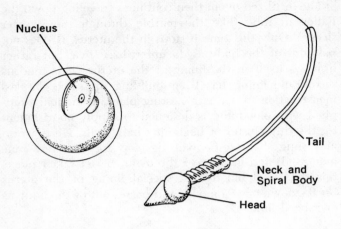

Figure 9
Ovum (egg cell)

Figure 10
Spermatozoon (sperm cell)

of cells. The sperm cells produce a special enzyme which dissolves this cementing substance. But there must be an enormous number of sperm all secreting the enzyme at once for conception to take place. That's why a man who produces too few sperm in an ejaculation is considered sterile. It may seem strange to say that a sperm count numbering in the millions may be considered low. Surely one out of so many sperm could manage to reach the ovum! But the problem arises because there isn't enough of the enzyme needed to make penetration of the ovum possible.[5]

Both ovum and sperm are extremely tiny. The *egg* cell is smaller than the period at the end of this sentence, and the sperm cell can be seen only with a microscope. Yet a thimbleful of sperm could father all the people now living—the total world population![6]

You'll notice the ovum is like a little ball with a center part called the *nucleus*. This contains the mother's portion of the hereditary make-up—her contribution toward the baby-to-be's eye and hair color, nose shape, body build, and inherited intelligence.

The tadpole-looking sperm cell has three parts: a head, which contains the hereditary material; the neck and "spiral body," which is the cell's energy-source, and a tail, which propels the cell as it travels in search of an ovum.

Every human cell is complete, having forty-six chromosomes—except the male sperm cell and the female ovum, which have twenty-three each. These two cells must meet and join to form a complete normal body cell of forty-six chromosomes. Chromosomes are minute bodies which carry the genes, the hereditary blueprint material.

The newly combined forty-six chromosomes will then be reproduced throughout the entire body of the child that has been conceived.

Our bodies contain millions of nerve, blood, bone and muscle cells. Yet each has a nucleus that is an exact duplicate of the first set of chromosomes that resulted when our father's sperm united with our mother's egg cell. It is this particular combination that provided the mold or pattern after which all the nuclei of all the cells in the body were modeled.[7] Every egg and sperm cell has a sex chromosome. In egg cells, it's always an X (female) chromosome. But among the twenty-three chromosomes in the head of a sperm cell, the sex chromosome may be *either* an X chromosome or a Y (male) chromosome. If a sperm cell with an X chromosome fertilizes an egg, the combination will be XX which produces a girl baby. If, on the other hand, there's a Y chromosome in the particular sperm that penetrates the ovum, the combination is XY, and the baby will be a boy. (You can remember the Y chromosome is the male one by thinking of the word "boy" which ends in "y.") In other words, the sex of a child comes from the father at the very moment of conception. It all depends on which sperm cell first reaches the ovum. As a point of interest, we receive half our inherited characteristics from our mothers and half from our fathers.

A Baby Develops

Approximately midway between a woman's menstrual periods, a ripened ovum is released from one of the ovaries. This process is called *ovulation.* Some women feel a slight pain when it happens. Some have slight bleeding (or "spotting"), but most women don't notice their time of ovulation. It has long been thought the ovaries alternate in the production of egg cells with the left ovary releasing an egg one month, the right ovary the alternate month. But this is not certain. Women who have had an ovary surgically removed can still release an egg each month from the one remaining ovary. It's also possible for both ovaries to release an egg at the time of ovulation, and if fertilization takes place, fraternal twins may result. This might also occur if a single ovary released two eggs instead of one.

Some women have a mistaken notion about ovulation. They believe eggs are released as part of sexual intercourse, and that eggs will be produced only if they reach the point of sexual *orgasm.* Women who want to have a baby sometimes worry themselves unnecessarily about this. They blame themselves and fear they will be barren if they're unable to have an orgasm. Probably the idea comes from knowing that ejaculation of sperm accompanies their husbands' orgasms, and they think it's a woman's orgasm that releases the ovum. However, ovulation in a woman is unrelated to sexual intercourse. Rather it's regulated by the pituitary gland and ovaries, and occurs regularly as part of the menstrual cycle.

After the egg cell leaves the ovary, it is picked up by

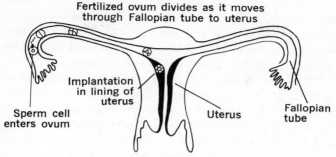

Fertilized ovum divides as it moves
through Fallopian tube to uterus

Implantation
in lining of
uterus

Sperm cell
enters ovum

Uterus

Fallopian
tube

Figure 11
How Conception Takes Place (Part 2)

the open end of the Fallopian tube and begins its journey toward the uterus. If pregnancy is going to occur,
the ovum must be fertilized within a day after its release.[8] A fertilized ovum continues through the tube,
traveling toward the uterus. The trip takes about three
or four days. Unfertilized ova disintegrate in the tube.

During sexual intercourse, the sperm cells are deposit-
ed at the upper end of a woman's vagina, near the cervi-
cal opening. Millions of tiny sperm swim up through the
uterus and into the Fallopian tubes, all racing toward
the prize, the ovum. The sperm, of course, have no way
of knowing whether an ovum is present or in which tube
it is. Those that swim up the empty tube are out of the
contest. But those which enter the tube which has just
received a released egg cell busy themselves trying to be
the first one to reach it. In one sense, the sperm cells are
competitors; in another they help each other. Earlier, we
saw they give off an enzyme designed to dissolve the
hard, outer layer or covering of the ovum so that penetration will be possible. Some scientists believe that
sperm cells bombard this outer layer, and with their combined impact "dent" it so that it may be more easily
broken through.[9]

At last one sperm succeeds. Its head and neck enter the egg; its nucleus moves toward the ovum's center to merge with the egg nucleus, forming a single cell of forty-six chromosomes. This is the moment of conception and the beginning of a potential human being.

When one sperm cell captures the prize, all runners-up have forever lost their chance. Only one sperm can enter an egg. At the moment of penetration a kind of protective shield, perhaps a chemical change in the membrane, makes it impossible for other sperm to claim the ovum. The winner loses its tail and settles down to a life in union with the egg. The losers, after a few hours, die and disintegrate.

Look closely at Figure 11 and notice what happens after the sperm unites with the ovum. The tiny cell begins to divide, first becoming two smaller cells, then four, and so on. This period of cleavage or cell division takes place during the three or four days the fertilized ovum is traveling down. Some physiologists describe its appearance as being like that of a tiny mulberry.[10]

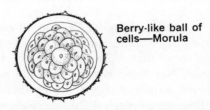

Berry-like ball of cells—Morula

Figure 12   "Mulberry" Stage of Cell Division

Look again at Figure 11 and notice what happens to the little cluster of cells. It becomes implanted in the lining of the specially prepared uterus. There it nestles into the cushiony membrane, richly supplied to insure its nourishment and growth.

As the *embryo* or growing fertilized egg develops, it is connected to its mother by means of a body stalk joined to the wall of the uterus. Through this stalk, food and oxygen from the mother's blood are carried to the embryo. Waste materials from the embryo are carried to the mother's bloodstream, eventually to be discharged from her body. The blood of the baby and of the mother, however, do not mix.

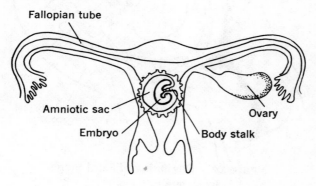

Figure 13
Development of Embryo in Early Stage

Over a period of time, the body stalk grows longer and becomes the *umbilical cord.* It is joined to the baby's abdomen at a point which, after birth, is called the navel. The other end of the umbilical cord is connected to a flat, pancake-like structure made up of tissues and blood vessels. This structure is the *placenta,* the organ attached to the uterus in the region where the fertilized ovum first implanted itself. Here, tiny blood vessels belonging to the mother and to the embryo lie close together. Through osmosis, nutrients from the mother's blood pass into the circulatory system of the developing infant, and in a reverse transfer process, the baby's waste products (such as carbon dioxide) are discharged.

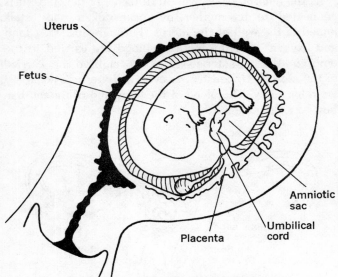

Figure 14   Beginning of Fetal Stage
Actual size at 2 months

After the first two months, the developing infant, no longer an embryo, is now called a *fetus*. Notice on Figure 14 the ways God has provided for comfort, protection, and nourishment of the fetus. One important provision that we haven't mentioned is the *amniotic sac* (sometimes referred to as "the bag of waters"). It's a protective elastic bag that forms around the developing infant. The fetus "floats" in fluid secreted from the inner lining of this sac. This protects the baby from bumps, jolts and pressures on the mother's body. In addition, it keeps him at just the right temperature.[11]

For about nine months, baby-to-be grows within the expanding uterus. During this time, all parts of his tiny body develop in readiness to leave his special home in the uterus.

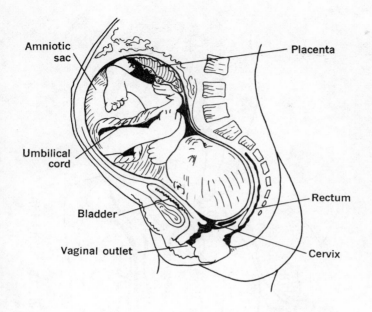

Amniotic
sac

Placenta

Umbilical
cord

Bladder

Rectum

Vaginal outlet

Cervix

Figure 15   Late Stage of Pregnancy

The process by which the baby enters the world is called childbirth or delivery. This involves some hard work on the part of the mother, and it's fitting to say she is "going into labor." There are muscular contractions of the uterus. The baby's head puts great pressure against the cervix (neck of the uterus), the woman pushes and "bears down," and eventually there is the wonderful moment of birth.

It isn't unusual for labor to last twelve to eighteen hours, although it may be either longer or shorter. Usually the delivery of the first child takes longer and may be more difficult than subsequent births.

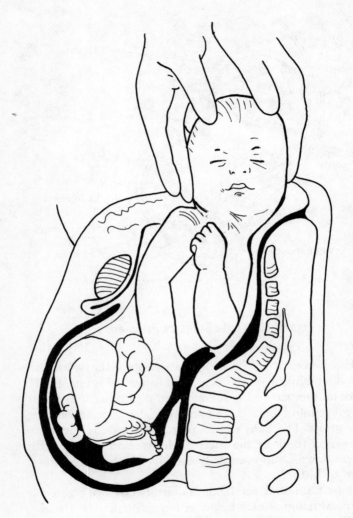

Figure 16   Childbirth

The final stage of labor is the expulsion of the *after-birth*—the placenta, amniotic sac, and certain membranes no longer needed. This is usually discharged about twenty minutes after birth.

One of the first things a doctor does when a baby is born is to tie off the umbilical cord about three inches above the point where it is attached to the baby. Then he cuts it, leaving just a tiny stump of the cord, which is treated to avoid infection. The stump dries and drops off within a week or two, leaving the little spot known as the navel or "belly button."

Helping Your Children Learn About Reproduction

Most children are naturally curious, and the human body ranks high on the list of things they're curious about. Also ranking high is the subject of babies and where they come from. These two combined interests make a good base on which to build a home sex education program. All you have to do is take advantage of your children's curiosity and then share with them sex information and attitudes related to the matters they're wondering about. You can share in a wise, simple, gradual and loving Christian framework.

There is, of course, no clear-cut timetable which children follow when asking a question about sex. A child might raise a question much sooner than you expect, or he may appear not to wonder about certain matters until later. But to give you a *general* idea of the kinds of questions children raise at different age levels, let's look at some typical questions of preschoolers, elementary school children, and junior high/high school students.

PRESCHOOL CHILDREN

Children under six are mostly concerned with body structure and function. They are also concerned with questions of their origin. Questions about body structure and function usually take the form of curiosity about differences in male and female organs. (You can explain this by saying God designed boys and girls differently so they could grow up to have the bodies of men and women and become fathers and mothers.)

"Why do women have breasts?" is a common question. You can reply that God made mothers' bodies so that they could make milk for their tiny babies. The milk is made in the breasts and is just right for babies. The breasts also have nipples so baby can suck comfortably as he is cuddled close to his mommy. Show your child a picture of a nursing mother. Or if you have a friend or relative who doesn't mind showing your child how this is done, let him watch. The scene can be presented as one of beauty and loving tenderness, something wonderful that has been planned by God. Of course, some mothers don't breast-feed their babies. Children can be told this is merely a matter of individual choice and that bottle-fed babies are also loved, cuddled, and have good, special milk.

Other questions about the body's structure and functions are often related to curiosity about *names*. "What's that?" "A penis"—or "a vulva," or "nipples," "breasts," "urine," "a bowel movement." A favorite question is "What is my belly button for?" You can reply that the navel is the place where he was connected to mommy in the special place inside her where he grew before being born. A special tube brought food and oxygen to the baby, and the navel is the spot where that tube was connected.

Preschoolers also want to know about babies. "Where do babies come from?" or "Where did you get me?" are frequent questions asked by preschoolers. You can explain that God has made a special snug, cozy place inside a mother's body called the *uterus*. Point to the lower part of your abdomen. There baby is fed and kept warm

130

and safe while he grows big and strong enough to come into the world.

Usually the next question is, "How does the baby come out of the mother?" Many children believe that babies are born through the navel. Tell your children God has designed a special passageway between the mother's legs for a baby to be born.

Occasionally, children ask if it hurts when the baby comes out. You can be honest but at the same time strive to avoid creating fears about childbirth. You can say, "Yes, there is some pain, because the muscles have to stretch very hard to let the baby come out. But doctors can help the woman so she doesn't hurt too much. Besides mothers are happy they're soon going to see the baby they've been carrying, and as soon as baby is born, they forget all about the pain."

Jesus talked about this when He told His disciples He would die on the cross. Jesus told them they would forget all their sadness and be glad because He would get up from the dead and they would see Him again. To help the disciples understand how things can hurt, and bring joy at the same time, Jesus said, "When a woman is about to give birth to a child she is sad, because her hour of suffering has come; but when the child is born she forgets her suffering, because she is happy that a baby has been born into the world" (John 16:21, *TEV*).

ELEMENTARY SCHOOL CHILDREN

In the lower grades, children's questions about reproduction continue to focus on the baby's origin, growth inside mother, and entrance into the world. When a small child asks how a baby gets started inside the mother, you needn't go into all the details of sexual intercourse. Usually a child will be satisfied with a simple explanation like this: "In a mother's body there are tiny egg cells. When a sperm cell from the father's body joins one

131

of these egg cells, a baby starts to grow inside the mother."

Questions about how the baby "eats" and "breathes" inside the mother can be answered from the material in this chapter. The baby doesn't "drown" in the amniotic sac because he gets his oxygen through the umbilical cord and not from air that must be breathed into the lungs. Questions about how the baby "knows when to come out" and how he gets out can be answered by a simple explanation of what happens in labor. God has designed the mother's body in such a way that when the baby is fully formed and ready to live in the outside world, the uterus will contract and push the baby out. If a child asks if it hurts the baby when the cord is cut, you can assure him it doesn't.

When children notice the increasing size of a pregnant woman and ask "why she's so fat," simply explain about the baby's development, growth and how the uterus stretches. You may want to show the child pictures in one of the many excellent children's books on gestation and reproduction.

In the upper elementary grades, children begin to ask more questions about conception. Earlier, they were satisfied to learn that the father's sperm and mother's ovum joined to produce a baby. Now the question becomes, "How does all this take place? How does the father put the sperm cell into the mother?" Again, it must be stressed there is no set age when this question may arise. Some children may be only six or seven years old. Others may be in fifth or sixth grade. The questions, however, usually occur in the same order: (1) Where do babies come from? (2) How do babies get started in the mother? and (3) How does the father put the sperm into the mother? This last one is the question that makes most parents fearful. It shouldn't. Simply explain that God designed the bodies of husbands and wives to fit together in a special way. Because husband and wife love and belong to each other, they become one body. Jesus said in marriage the husband and wife are "one flesh." The sperm cells that meet the egg cells in order for babies to start to grow are produced in the little sac between the father's legs. The father places his penis inside a special opening in the mother's body so that the sperm cells can swim up to the place where the egg cell is. This happens while the husband and wife lie close to each other.

As children ask more details, be prepared to furnish as much information as you sense is needed at a particular time.

Questions directly related to *reproduction* are these: *Does a baby grow in a woman every time the husband and wife have sexual intercourse?* Answer: No. There are only a few days each month when it is possible for an egg cell to be fertilized. Most often there is no egg cell waiting in the Fallopian tubes when the sperm cells swim up to meet it.

Can people who aren't married have babies? The answer is, yes; because a man and woman can have sexual intercourse without being married. But this isn't pleasing to God. Ask your child why he thinks God wants people to be married before they have babies. Stress the need for love and care of a child within a family setting.

If a wife is already pregnant, can she and her husband still have intercourse? Could another baby be conceived then? Most physicians tell couples they may continue sex relations up to about six weeks before the baby is due. Pregnant women do not conceive because hormones prevent ovulation.

When children ask whether a baby will be a boy or a girl, or what sperm and ova look like, explain by showing the drawings in this chapter. The section on *Multiple*

Births in chapter 8 will help answer question about twins and triplets.

JUNIOR HIGH AND HIGH SCHOOL STUDENTS

Younger teens may ask many of the questions just discussed. Older teens will focus on matters of ethics and their own personal social lives. Most older teens understand basic facts about sex and reproduction, or at least *think* they do. If you're getting a late start with sex education, you might want to discuss the three chapters on the physiology of sex and reproduction with your teenagers. But if you have gradually taught them over the years, you'll probably find teens more concerned with dating, necking, petting, masturbation, what's right and wrong with premarital sex and how can people know they're "in love."

Teens also wonder how a woman and her doctor know the date when the baby will arrive. No one can predict with absolute accuracy the date of birth, but predictions can come close. The period from conception to birth is about nine months, or 270-280 days. Most doctors ask the mother-to-be when her last menstrual period began. To this date, they add seven days and count back three months and add a year. The date arrived at should be close to the infant's birthday.

Older children ask why some people can't have children, or how couples control fertility. For answers to these questions, see *Birth Control (Contraception)* and *Sterility and Sterilization* in chapter 8. One category of questions raised by junior highs and high schoolers is the matter of unusual circumstances or problems relating to birth. The following information may be helpful:

Birth defects. Researchers are making significant progress in understanding what happens during pregnancy to cause babies to be born with mental and physical handicaps.[12] Some defect problems are inherited and pass from

134

one generation to another. Other defects result from diseases a mother contracted during pregnancy. Rubella (German or three-day measles) is one of the worst offenders. This disease can cause blindness, deafness and mental defects.

Rh factor (blood difference between husband and wife) can cause death and/or deformity among babies. If a mother's blood is tested and observed for antibodies during pregnancy, a doctor can usually treat the problem. Another cause of birth defects is damage to the fetus from drugs and medicines. The Thalidomide tragedy emphasized the importance of great caution with regard to medication during pregnancy. Mothers who took Thalidomide as a tranquilizer during pregnancy bore babies with severe deformities. They were usually born without arms and legs.

Persons born with *birth marks* (skin blemishes, or disfigurements) have nothing to do with the mother seeing or dreaming something bad during pregnancy. This is an old superstition with no basis in fact. The marks occur because parts of the skin didn't develop normally during gestation. A certain area may contain an unusual amount of pigmentation or an excess of blood vessels. Some birthmarks can be removed by plastic surgery; others can be covered by cosmetics.

A *breech birth* is a birth in which the baby is born buttocks first instead of headfirst. Most babies are born with the head facing downward. This is the first part to emerge from the mother's vagina. But in about three percent of births, the baby lies in the uterus in an upright position, with his buttocks, legs, and feet ready to come out first.[13] These births are more difficult for mother and child, but with good medical care there is little to worry about. (The word "breech" is another name for the buttocks.)

A *Cesarean section* is a surgical procedure in which a

135

baby is delivered through an incision made in his mother's abdomen and uterus. Sometimes conditions make normal childbirth inadvisable or unsafe. The doctor will recommend surgical delivery. Subsequent Cesarean sections depends on the *reason* for the first. Some women have later babies in the normal way, even though the first may have been born Cesarean. The name "Cesarean" comes from Julius Caesar who is reputed to have been born by means of such an operation.

A *miscarriage* occurs when a baby is expelled from the mother's uterus before it has developed enough to live. Technically, a miscarriage is the loss of the fetus between the fourth and sixth months of pregnancy. If the embryo is discharged during the first three months, the occurrence is called an involuntary, spontaneous abortion. Some causes for termination of the pregnancy are not fully understood. Sometimes the ovum or sperm are defective or something didn't go right during the stage of implantation.

A *premature birth.* Doctors consider a baby premature when he is born before full-term, (before the full nine months) or when he weighs less than five and a half pounds. Unlike cases discussed above, a premature infant, or "preemie," is fully developed but he requires special care, including some time spent in an incubator.

Methods and Materials for Helping
Youngsters Learn About Reproduction

New additions to a family provide excellent opportunities to help your other children learn about babies. If you have a child of two or three, you'll want him to know a new baby is coming and be looking forward to the time when he arrives. Telling about the baby's coming *too* early in the pregnancy makes the wait interminably long to a small child. But as the time grows nearer you'll want your other child or children to share in the fun of shopping or getting a tiny bed ready. This is a difficult moment for your young child and he needs much loving reassurance that he isn't being replaced by a new model. Advance knowledge that Mommy will spend some time in the hospital when she gets the baby is also wise. A helpful way to make this clear is to talk about the time of his or her own birth. An excellent little story book that helps you do this is *The Day You Were Born* by Evelyn Swetnam (a Whitman Tell-A-Tale Book). It begins with a brief description of what it was like inside the mother, then tells what it is like to be born, cared for by the nurses and doctors in the hospital, and loved by a mother and father. Other inexpensive children's books are especially intended to prepare little ones for the birth of a sibling. Two "Little Golden Books" that preschoolers will enjoy hearing you read to them are *New Brother, New Sister* by Jean Fiedler and *Jenny's New Brother* by Elaine Evans.

Small children are thrilled to know a baby is growing inside their mother. It's a special, wonderful secret. In the latter part of the pregnancy, it's especially exciting to place one's hand on Mommy's abdomen and feel the baby kick! Then, when the baby arrives, your older child can watch during breast-feeding and can also help in powdering and diapering the baby. All of these occasions provide excellent and natural opportunities for wholesome sex education.

Since children are great imitators and like to play "let's pretend," don't be surprised or alarmed if they sometimes act out some of the new things they learn about reproduction and male/female body differences. Children may pat their tummies and say a baby is growing inside, or they might pretend they're nursing a doll or teddy bear "like Mommy feeds the baby."

A little girl might try to find out what it feels like to urinate standing up. Other children are curious about each other and sometimes examine each other's genitals. Onlooking parents find it difficult to see things the way tiny children do. Many parents become fearful and unreasonably harsh. "Don't you ever play with that dirty little boy again! How could you ever let him touch you like that? Naughty, naughty child! You're going to be punished." "You are a very bad little boy (girl)! The very idea—taking your clothes off outside! And letting everybody see what you look like! Shame on you!"

It will help to realize that all children are curious and this is a normal and natural part of growing up. Furthermore, you can teach children the importance of modesty and privacy without conveying shame. You will be surprised to see how—even apart from such efforts—children develop their own sense of modesty, especially by the time they are ready for kindergarten and first grade.

If you feel your child is a bit too uninhibited, you can teach him that there are certain parts of the body that are very special and most people keep them covered with clothing. Also, it isn't good manners to perform private functions of the body (like urination) outside in public view. The child should come inside and use the bathroom instead. Most children easily grasp these instructions because they observe such customs among the adults they like to imitate.

Sex curiosity and sex play among young children aren't unusual or unnatural and need not cause parents to panic. (See "Talk It Over" section at the end of this chapter.) On the other hand, this isn't to suggest that such play should be encouraged. Use any incidents of this sort as occasions to talk over questions your child may have about sex, and then calmly direct him to other acceptable play activities.

Object lessons like seeing a pregnant woman, a nursing mother or a newborn baby, can be a great aid in sex education. Also watching birds build their nests and prepare for their babies is a wonderful story about the ongoingness of *life*. Children are glad to be alive, and they like to know how other things like animals, plants, fish and birds "come alive." E. Margaret Clarkson's warm and fascinating book, *Susie's Babies* (Eerdmans) combines a Christian emphasis with an animal-world observation of sex education.

Sometimes parents hesitate to compare human and animal reproduction for fear children will get the idea that man is just an animal. Most books, however, take great pains to show how humans differ from animals, even though their bodies have things in common. One fine book that does this is Karl de Schweinitz's book for grade-school children, entitled *Growing Up—How We Become Alive, Are Born, and Grow* (Macmillan).

We've been thinking about observation and object lessons as tools in sex education. You might want to consider taking your children to see a display on human reproduction found in some museums. Chicago's famed Museum of Science and Industry has a display of actual fetuses that have been preserved, showing the exact size for every month of pregnancy. (You can explain to the children that these babies were not able to live because something went wrong during the pregnancy and they couldn't grow to be live babies.) Other illustrations or object lessons are those you can make yourself. For example, Ruth Hummel in the book *Wonderfully Made* (Concordia) suggests that children do an experiment in order to understand how the amniotic sac cushions the baby from jolts and bumps. She suggests that children put a small ball into a balloon and then fill the balloon with water. The children will find the ball moves away from their hands as they push into the balloon, because it's protected by the water.

The following are some of the many excellent books on

139

reproduction written and illustrated especially for children.

FOR PRESCHOOLERS
The Story of You by Edgar and Ada Cockefair (Monona Publications)

KINDERGARTEN THROUGH SECOND GRADE
A Baby Is Born by Milton I. Levine, M.D., and Jean H. Seligmann (Golden Press)

I Wonder, I Wonder by Marguerite Kurth Frey (Concordia)

The Beginning of Life by Eva Knox Evans (Macmillan, Crowell-Collier Press)

GRADES THREE AND FOUR
The Wonderful Story of How You Were Born by Sidonie Matsner Gruenberg (Doubleday)

Susie's Babies by E. Margaret Clarkson (Eerdmans)

Growing Up by Karl de Schweinitz (Macmillan)

GRADES FIVE AND SIX
A Story About You by Marion O. Lerrigo and Helen Southard (American Medical Association)

Wonderfully Made by Ruth Hummel (Concordia)

JUNIOR HIGH
Love and Sex in Plain Language by Eric W. Johnson (Bantam Pathfinder paperback)

Volume 2 (on reproduction), *The Life Cycle Library for Young People* (Parent and Child Institute)

Take the High Road (Chapter 2) by A. J. Bueltmann (Concordia)

Facts About Sex by Sol Gordon (John Day Co.)—excellent pictures of gestation and childbirth

The Miracle of Life (American Medical Association)
Love, Sex, and Being Human by Paul Bohannan
(Doubleday paperback)

COLLEGE AND YOUNG ADULT
Reproduction, Sex and Preparation for Marriage by
Lawrence Q. Crawley, James L. Malfetti, Ernest I.
Stewart, and Nina Vas Dias (Prentice-Hall paperback)
Your First Pregnancy (pamphlet available for 10¢ from
Kimberly-Clark Corp.)

Let's Talk It Over

1. Human reproduction is often referred to in Scripture; sometimes as poetic description or as a means of illustrating spiritual truths. At other times, it is simply and frankly descriptive. Look up the following passages and relate them to the material in this chapter: Jeremiah 13:21; Galatians 4:19; Isaiah 45:10; Romans 8:22; Genesis 25:21-26; Genesis 38:27-30; John 3:3-8; Exodus 1:15-19; Job 3:1-16; Psalm 139:13-16; Ecclesiastes 11:5; Isaiah 26:17; Isaiah 42:14; Isaiah 49:15; Ezekiel 16:4; Isaiah 66:10-13.

2. Make a list of questions on reproduction you would find hard to discuss with your children. Why would they seem difficult? Discuss and try to decide how you would answer each one should it arise.

3. In your own words, describe conception, gestation and childbirth. Use the drawings in this chapter to aid you in your description. Make sure all the details are clear in your own mind so that you'll be prepared for the questions children may ask at different age levels.

4. Diane is the mother of two boys; Phil—four, and three-month-old Nathan. One day when Diane was looking for Phil, she found him in the garage with a three-year-old neighbor girl. As she approached, the two children

hurried out nervously. "What are you children up to?" she asked. The little girl ran away, but Phil replied innocently, "Jenny took down her panties so I could see what she looks like." Diane's first impulse was to show shock and disapproval, but she had read enough about small children to know better. She smiled and said, "Oh, what did you see?" "Jenny doesn't have a penis," answered Phil. "She looks different than me and Nathan."

"Yes," said Diane, matter-of-factly, "God made little girls' bodies one way and little boys' bodies another way."

"But how can Jenny go to the bathroom?" asked Phil with a wrinkled brow.

"All girls have a special opening between their legs, and sit down on the toilet instead of standing up when they urinate." Phil's curiosity was satisfied and his interests quickly focused on the aroma from the kitchen. "We're having soup, aren't we, Mommy? Goodie! I'm so hungry! Jenny and I played restaurant this morning. She made soup out of water and rose petals, and I made hamburgers out of mud!" he grinned, and Diane tousled his hair and hugged him close.

Discuss this story. Did Diane handle the matter wisely? Why or why not? Pretend you are *Jenny's* mother and Jenny comes home and reports the incident to you. Role-play what might be the reaction if Jenny's mother handles it (a) calmly and wisely, and then (b) in an unwise manner.

References

1. Lawrence Q. Crowley, James L. Malfetti, Ernest I. Stewart, and Nina Vas Dias, *Reproduction, Sex, and Preparation for Marriage* (Englewood Cliffs, N.J.: Prentice-Hall Inc., 1964), pp. 19, 36.

2. Estimates on the exact number of undeveloped egg cells range from 50,000 to 400,000. See Crawley, et al., p.

14; Justus J. Schifferes, *Family Medical Encyclopedia* (New York: Perma Books, Inc., 1959), p. 465; C. E. Turner, *Personal and Community Health* (Saint Louis: C. V. Mosby Co., 1967), p. 75; Fred E. D'Amour, *Basic Physiology* (Chicago: The University of Chicago Press, 1961), p. 472. Bohannan points out that current research leads some scientists to believe that, contrary to what has been thought in the past, it may be possible for a woman to manufacture additional eggs during adulthood. Others disagree and are yet of the opinion that all egg cells are already present at birth. See Paul Bohannan, *Love, Sex and Being Human* (New York: Doubleday paperback, 1970), p. 22.

3. Eric W. Johnson, *Love and Sex in Plain Language* (New York: Bantam Pathfinder paperback edition, 1968), p. 13.

4. Schifferes' *Family Medical Encyclopedia*, p. 492; Crawley, et al., p. 8.

5. D'Amour, *Basic Psysiology*, p. 493.

6. Crawley, et al., p. 8.

7. The American Medical Association, *The Miracle of Life* (Chicago: AMA, 1970), p. 13.

8. Crawley, et al., p. 18; Bohannan, p. 22.

9. Crawley, et al., p. 37.

10. American Medical Association, *Miracle of Life*, p. 13.

11. Schifferes' *Family Medical Encyclopedia*, p. 412.

12. Much of this information was taken from the pamphlet, "Mission Possible—Birth Defects Prevention," published by the National Foundation—March of Dimes, 1971.

13. Crawley, et al., p. 76.

CHAPTER EIGHT

What If a Child Asks About...?

It's a matter of common parental concern today that the mass media exposes children to a wide range of sex-related subjects. Because of this, today's children may raise questions beyond the usual facts of life.

This chapter helps parents prepare for questions like "What's a homosexual?" "What does 'abortion' mean?" "Why do some women become prostitutes?" "What's rape?" "What does it mean when a newspaper says a man was arrested for 'indecent exposure'?" "What does family planning mean?"

For easy reference, each of these topics is arranged alphabetically to provide *parents* with basic, general information on each subject.

Abortion

An abortion occurs when a pregnancy is interrupted and the embryo or fetus is expelled from the uterus before the developing baby is able to live on its own. There are *natural* or *spontaneous* abortions which, for reasons not fully understood, the body rids itself of the embryo

145

—usually during the second or third month of pregnancy. Such involuntary abortions are sometimes called *miscarriages,* although technically that term is reserved for unintentional abortions occurring during the fourth to sixth months of pregnancy.

When most people talk about abortions, however, they usually mean *induced* abortions, performed through a surgical procedure. The contents of the uterus (fetus, placenta and tissue) are removed and the pregnancy is terminated. If the pregnancy is in the early stages (up until twelve weeks), the operation is usually performed through the vagina. The cervix is stretched (dilated) and the contents of the uterus are removed through scraping the uterine walls with a special knife called a curette. This procedure is sometimes used after an incomplete natural abortion. It is familiarly known as a "D and C" (dilation and curettage). An abortion also can be carried out through the vagina by means of a special vacuum pump. If a pregnancy is interrupted after thirteen weeks, the usual procedure is through an incision of the abdomen and uterus.[1]

Induced abortions may be either *therapeutic* (performed legally and under professional medical care) or *criminal* (performed illegally, often in highly unsanitary conditions and by persons without medical training, with great risk to the mother). One reason for the concern about liberalizing abortion laws in recent years was a desire to prevent the terrible toll of death, sterility and other complications that came from desperate women seeking criminal abortionists.

Up until the Supreme Court decision of 1973 which swept aside anti-abortion laws, states varied greatly in their regulation of abortion. Some permitted the operation only if the mother's life were in danger. Other states permitted abortion in cases involving the physical or mental well-being of the mother, or where the pregnancy resulted from rape or incest, or where there was a distinct possibility that the child would be deformed (such as if the mother contracted German measles during early pregnancy or where tests revealed genetic problems).

A United States Supreme Court ruling in 1973 declared that the Constitutional guarantee of privacy makes the termination of pregnancy a matter to be decided by the individual woman concerned. It is up to her and her doctor—not the state. States may not make laws forbidding abortion during the first six months of pregnancy; although after the third month, they have the right to step in with regulations and safeguards for the protection of the woman's health. States are permitted, however, to make laws preventing termination of pregnancy after the sixth month, because from that point on the fetus is presumed to be capable of living outside the mother's uterus. Up until that time, according to the Supreme Court, the rights of the fetus are not protected by the Constitution, the wording of which applies to postnatal life only. "In short," wrote Justice Harry Blackmun in the majority opinion, "the unborn have never been recognized in the law as persons in the whole sense."

There are sharp differences among Christians with regard to abortion. Some consider it murder; others say the operation might be an act of mercy. Some believe that the soul enters the fetus at conception. Others feel the zygote (fertilized ovum) is just a cell that may become a *potential* human being but is not yet one at the moment and hence its removal is not "murder." The Bible is silent on the subject, although some Christians believe Exodus 21:22,23 may indicate a developing embryo or fetus was not regarded as a *full* human being, since inflicting an injury on a pregnant woman which resulted in its loss was to be punished by a fine rather than by death, under the "life for life" law.

In 1968, in an effort to put the matter of abortion in

147

Christian perspective, the Christian Medical Society and *Christianity Today* sponsored a conference of leading evangelical scholars in medicine, genetics, psychology, sociology, law and theology. Their conclusions are now published under the title *Birth Control and the Christian.* Another excellent book providing guidance for the Christian is R. F. R. Gardner's *Abortion: The Personal Dilemma.*[2]

Talking About Abortion with Your Children

Most preschoolers, who happen to overhear something about someone having an abortion would not understand and might even become upset if you tried to explain. Perhaps a simple, "Oh, it means she has to have an operation at the hospital," would satisfy the child's curiosity.

Children of elementary school age (especially older ones) are able to understand that sometimes "something goes wrong" so that a woman isn't able to carry a pregnancy through to completion. Perhaps they have seen a television drama that has presented the dangers of a criminal abortion, or the terrible anguish of parents faced with the possibility of a deformed child. Christian parents should discuss these matters openly and relate them to their own values.

Teen-agers may be interested to know more of the physical details of how an abortion is performed. Because of the widespread discussion of abortion, it is not unusual for them to know of someone who stopped an illegitimate pregnancy by getting an abortion. Teens are also interested in many of the ethical aspects of abortion and need guidance in the light of Christian principles. It is especially important for teen-agers to see that abortion is not something to be taken lightly, and should not be regarded casually as a convenient escape hatch for promiscuity.

Adoption

Adoption is the act of choosing and taking as one's own a child born of other parents. Each state has adoption laws and agencies staffed by persons trained in placing children in homes where they will be loved and cared for by parents who want to welcome them into their homes to be their very own children. Some people adopt children because they are unable to have any of their own. Others are concerned about the world's population problems and believe it may be more important to care for children already here than to bring other children into the world. Many people want to love children who have been traditionally hard to place, older, handicapped, or children of racially mixed parentage. Some states now permit unmarried persons to adopt.

Talking About Adoption with Your Children

Parents of adopted children have special problems when discussing sex and reproduction. They cannot read them a story telling how Mommy and Daddy loved each other and how a sperm from Daddy and an egg from Mommy came together in Mommy's body and grew to be the child. Instead, they tell about the time the child was lovingly chosen and joined the family after birth. They may want to use a special children's book, such as Valentina Wasson's *The Chosen Baby*.[3] Sooner or later, however, the child comes to realize that he had a different mother, but can be assured that his present mother is his "real" mother, the one who loves and cares for him and to whom he belongs completely.

Preschoolers often have trouble reconciling the facts of birth with the facts of adoption. Even when they do understand that they grew within another woman's body, they may find they have difficulty accepting the fact that a mother would give up her little baby. Thus, they often make up stories about their biological parents dying and

149

leaving them behind to be cared for by someone else. Eda LeShan, in her helpful pamphlet *You and Your Adopted Child*,[4] points out this is not unusual and such thoughts are comforting to small children whose imaginations turn to make-believe in an effort to assure themselves they were not given up because of some defect. Actually, Mrs. LeShan points out, when small children ask, "How did I get here?" what they are most concerned about is, "Are you glad I'm here?" It is the warm, accepting love of the parents for their adopted child that provides the climate he needs to grow up with, for a sense of confidence and self-esteem.[5] An adopted child, like any other child, needs to know his parents consider him a special gift of God.

Sometimes school-age children who are adopted need added reassurance. Mrs. LeShan's booklet describes one family's wise handling of their son's distress when his schoolmates taunted him with ugly remarks about being "a bastard." The parents explained the meaning of the word and assured him that even if a child is born out of wedlock he isn't any different than any other child. And furthermore, when he's adopted he is the legal child of his new parents.[6] They provided him with the loving understanding and reinforcement he needed at a difficult time.

During the teen-age years, an adopted child may do a great deal of thinking about his birth, his biological parents, and the matter of illegitimacy. When he hears warnings about the evils of premarital sex, he may wonder if his own parents were "immoral" and fear that he might be a "child of sin" and come from a "bad background." Here again, parents must show love, patience, understanding, and realism. Christians know that *all* persons sin (Romans 3:23). Even if the child *was* conceived as the result of premarital intercourse, it doesn't mean his parents were terribly wicked in some special way.

Many young people—even Christian young people—make mistakes and lose control of their drives. This is certainly not beyond the scope of God's grace and forgiveness. Furthermore, adopted children can be assured that the natural mother must have wanted the best for her baby for her to place him in a home where he would be loved and cared for with pride and joy. There is no reason for a child to torture himself with thoughts that he came from a "bad" mother.

Adopted children may be delighted to see how God uses the analogy of adoption in talking about the way we are placed into His family through faith in Christ. Paul tells us that we are God's very own children, adopted into His family and that the "Holy Spirit speaks to us deep in our hearts, and tells us that we really are God's children. And since we are his children, we will share his treasures—for all God gives to his Son Jesus is now ours too" (Romans 8:16-17, *TLB*). (Also see Galatians 4:5-7.)

Adultery

The term "adultery" refers to sexual unfaithfulness. When a married man or a married woman engage in sexual intercourse with someone other than the spouse, they commit adultery and violate the seventh commandment (Exodus 20:14,17; Leviticus 18:20; Job 31:9-11; Proverbs 6:27-32; 7:6-23). The Bible makes clear that adultery is a sin—for both men and women (see Hosea 4:13,14; Leviticus 20:10; Deuteronomy 22:22; Mark 7:20-23; Romans 7:1-3; Malachi 2:13-15; 1 Corinthians 6:9; Hebrews 13:4). It is not only a sin against one's neighbor, but according to Genesis 20:6; 39:9, *a sin against God.*

Jesus taught that one can commit adultery in the thought-life even if one does not engage in the actual act (Matthew 5:27,28). (See Sex Thoughts and Fantasies in this chapter.) However, as with any other sin, the person who is truly repentant and seeks God's forgiveness can experience restoration, cleansing and spiritual healing. The well-known story of David and Bathsheba in 2 Samuel 11:2—12:25 illustrates this point. But note David's sincere repentance and remorse in telling Nathan the prophet that the sin had really been against God; this same thought is also captured in David's prayer for forgiveness in Psalm 51. Another illustration of God's mercy after an act of adultery is the story of the woman brought to Jesus by the Pharisees who wanted to stone her (John 8:1-11).

Talking with Your Children About Adultery

With preschoolers, you can point out that when a man and a woman get married, they promise to belong to each other in a special way. This means they will, as God planned, leave their own mothers and fathers and start a home of their own as husband and wife. But sometimes people break that promise. The man may want to spend his time with a woman who isn't his wife. Or a woman may want to give her love and attention to a man who isn't her husband.

A similar approach may be used to answer grade-school children. Depending upon their age and stage of sex knowledge, it may be well to be more explicit and say, "Adultery means that a married person is having sex relations with somebody other than the one he or she is married to."

Teen-agers understand the implications of adultery and parents should discuss what the Scriptures have to say about this. Passages such as Jeremiah 3:20 and James 4:4 show how marital unfaithfulness is an illustration of spiritual unfaithfulness.

Artificial Insemination

In the procedure called *artificial insemination,* semen is injected into a woman's vagina artificially. Through the use of a syringe, a physician places the semen (the thick fluid containing the sperm cells) at the opening of the cervix (the neck of the uterus). The usual reason for this is infertility when the husband has a low sperm count. But in some cases semen is injected artificially because the wife's body characteristics make conception by normal means impossible.

There are two forms of artificial insemination, AIH (artificial insemination, husband) and AID (artificial insemination, donor). In cases where the semen is provided by the husband, semen is collected from several ejaculations and injected at one time in order to make the sperm count higher. In cases where the semen is provided by a donor, much counseling is needed beforehand. There are medical considerations, such as the donor's Rh factor, genetic background, efforts to match as closely as possible such matters as the husband's complexion, hair color, and other characteristics. There are psychological and emotional matters to consider. How will the husband feel toward a child that is not biologically his own? There are also legal factors to consider. Even though the donor remains anonymous and signs away all legal rights, there have been court cases involving inheritance rights. Because each state has different laws regarding artificial insemination, the husband is urged to legally adopt the baby.

In addition, there are the moral considerations. Many Christians have no objection to artificial insemination if the semen has come from the husband. But questions and doubts are raised if the procedure utilizes the semen of an unknown donor. For many Christians, this method of solving the problem of childlessness seems to be nothing short of "legalized adultery." But other Christians view it simply as a medical procedure that permits a couple to know the joys of pregnancy, childbirth and the possibility of having a child that has the biological inheritance of at least one parent. In contrast, adoption provides no *biological* relationship. One outstanding Christian geneticist said:

"I don't think the adultery argument (against artificial insemination) can be defended from the Bible. Jesus stressed the idea that lustful desire is the essential point of adultery. Going back to the Old Testament, you'll find that the Levite Law of marriage in which a near kinsman of a dead man is obligated to father an heir for the widow is a form of donor insemination, though not artificial."[7]

Talking with Your Children
About Artificial Insemination

The subject is not likely to come up with preschoolers, but elementary children may ask about it in connection with a newspaper or magazine article that refers to "test-tube babies," the name sometimes given to children conceived by artificial insemination. Or children may ask about it when they hear someone talking about breeding animals this way. Should they ask if it's possible for humans to have children this way, you can tell them it is and that married couples sometimes ask a doctor to help them have a baby through artificial insemination when they cannot have one in the usual way.

Birth Control (Contraception)

Through birth control or family planning, couples limit the size of their families and plan how far apart they would like births to be. Most married couples use some form of birth control to reduce the risk of a new baby every year and the corresponding problems of a large family. Limiting and planning the size of one's family is to be aware of the mother's physical and emotional well-being, financial and housing needs, plus the general welfare of the whole family.

Measures used to prevent conception are spoken of as "contraception" (from the Latin word *contra* which means "against, in opposition to"). Perhaps the most talked about and most effective contraceptives are *oral contraceptives*. "The Pill" (taken by mouth) prevents conception by stopping the woman from producing a ripe egg (ovulating). These should be prescribed by a physician and taken according to his instructions. Another method of contraception used by women is the IUD (intra-uterine device). These devices are small loops or coils that are inserted into a woman's uterus by a physician, who fits it according to the size of the woman's uterus. The IUD is kept in place for as long as the woman wishes not to become pregnant. If she decides otherwise, a physician can simply remove it.

The diaphragm-with-jelly method is another common and reliable means of birth control. A diaphragm is a soft rubber cap-like device encircled by a rubber-covered flexible spring. It must be fitted by a physician, but unlike the IUD it is not kept in place all the time. Before sexual intercourse a woman inserts the diaphragm with her finger or an inserter. When the diaphragm is pushed up through the vagina and into place, it covers the opening of the cervix and prevents the husband's sperm from entering the uterus. The diaphragm must be used with a sperm-destroying jelly or cream and left in place for at least eight hours after intercourse. A diaphragm is not felt by either husband or wife during their sexual relations. Sometimes spermicidal jellies, creams and foams are used without a diaphragm. These are easily purchased in most drugstores and when used properly often work fairly well. They are certainly better than nothing, but when used alone they are not nearly as reliable as the diaphragm method.

A method of birth control in which the husband takes the responsibility is through the use of the condom.

Sometimes called "rubbers" (or referred to by their trade names such as "Trojans" or "Sheiks"), they look somewhat like a narrow uninflated toy balloon or like the finger of a rubber glove. Designed to fit over an erect penis, they are put into place before sexual intercourse so that the ejaculation does not spurt semen into the woman's vagina. Carefully used, the condom will not tear or slip off, and is an effective contraceptive. However, some husbands and wives find the method unsatisfactory because the penis and vagina are not in direct contact. Also the "afterglow" period is cut short since the husband must withdraw the penis from his wife's vagina immediately after ejaculation so that the condom may be removed before the erection is lost.

Some couples use no chemicals or mechanical devices, but instead use the *rhythm method.* This is the traditional method advocated by the Roman Catholic Church which holds that all other methods are "unnatural" and therefore wrong. The rhythm method is based on the fact that a woman is only able to become pregnant during a few days each month—the time around her ovulation. The couple then abstains from sex relations during that time. However, since it is difficult to know the exact time of ovulation and since many women are highly irregular in their menstrual cycle, the rhythm method has a much greater pregnancy risk than many other methods.

Two highly unreliable methods are *withdrawal* in which the husband removes the penis from the vagina just before ejaculation and *douching,* flushing out the vagina with water or other liquid just after intercourse. There are many research efforts currently underway to find even better methods of contraception than are available at present.

Not many decades ago Christians thought that birth control was sinful and contrary to the will of God. Most Protestants and a great number of Catholics now believe that it is an important part of family responsibility to wisely plan and time their births. Most Protestants feel it is the *motive*, not the *method*, that must be considered and disagree with the Roman Catholic position that rhythm is the only method permissible if a couple wishes to please God. A few Christians feel the withdrawal method (*coitus interruptus*) is sinful on the basis of Genesis 38:8-10, although Onan's sin was not a contraceptive method but his failure to fulfill the requirement of providing a child for his brother's widow. There are also some Christians who are hesitant about the use of the IUD, since it is possible that what the device does is to prevent fertilized ova from burrowing into the lining of the uterus. They feel this is a type of abortion. For further guidance read: *Birth Control and the Christian*[8] and/or *Planned Parenthood* (Planned Parenthood and Birth Control in the Light of Christian Ethics).[9]

Talking with Your Children About Birth Control

The subject is not likely to arise with preschoolers. Elementary school children, however, are alert enough to be aware of the current concern over "population explosion" and know that families are being urged to limit their size. An eight-year-old might surprise you with a comment like, "She should be taking birth control pills." The idea that a mother takes special pills to keep from having too many babies or having them too close together is the method most easily understood by young children.

Teen-agers are well aware of birth control and are deeply concerned with world population problems. (One high school had a special fund-raising project for Planned Parenthood.) Nevertheless, many teens and college students have a hazy idea about how contraception works, and what is and is not reliable. Some have tried soda-pop douches and Saran-Wrap condoms with tragic

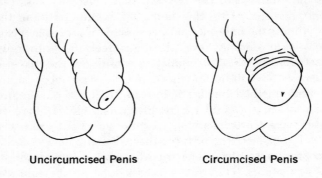

Uncircumcised Penis   Circumcised Penis

Figure 17   Penis

results. Parents who have an open relationship with their teen-agers should talk freely about right and wrong methods of contraception. This is certainly not to suggest that teens use such methods and therefore feel free to engage in premarital sex! Christian sex ethics are not built upon fear of pregnancy but upon the revealed will of God.

Circumcision

Circumcision is a minor surgical procedure in which the foreskin is removed from a penis. The operation usually takes place during the first few days after birth, at a time when healing takes place quickly with minimum discomfort to the baby. Figure 17 shows how an uncircumcised penis and a circumcised penis differ in appearance.

During Bible times, circumcision was performed for religious reasons, and this continues to be the reason for the circumcision of Jewish males today. Other males are circumcised for reasons of hygiene. It makes it easier to keep the penis clean and is a precaution against irritation, inflammation and disease that sometimes occur through bacteria in the glandular secretion that may collect under the foreskin. Most doctors in our country today recommend routine circumcision on all baby boys, rather than risking the need for a complex and painful operation later.

Other doctors disagree and do not see a necessity for circumcision except for medical reasons where the need is clearly evident in the individual case (such as when the foreskin adheres to the head of the penis). This, for example, is the outlook of many European physicians. Expectant parents should discuss in advance with their physician whether or not their baby (if it is a boy) should be circumcised.

There is no evidence that circumcision either decreases or increases sexual pleasure in marriage.[10] Some medical authorities, however, are of the opinion that it does enhance sensual enjoyment to some degree.[11]

Many cultures throughout the world practice circumcision as part of their puberty rites, signifying a boy's initiation into manhood and preparation for marriage. For the Israelites, circumcision was God's appointed sign of the covenant He made with Abraham. And according to Genesis 17:10-12 it was to be performed on eight-day-old baby boys. This was to be an outward sign of an inward relationship to God. But without the inner "heart circumcision" the outward sign meant nothing (Deuteronomy 30:6; 10:16; Jeremiah 4:4; Romans 2:28,29). Both Jesus and Paul were circumcised as eight-day-old infants under Jewish law (Luke 2:21; Philippians 3:5).

During Old Testament times, even though some of Israel's neighbors practiced circumcision, there were others like the Philistines (1 Samuel 17:36; 18:25) who did not. Gradually, the term "uncircumcised" came to be ap-

159

plied to all Gentiles, or "heathen," who were outside God's special covenant with Abraham. There was much confusion and dissension in the early church about whether all Christian males were required to be circumcised. Not for hygienic reasons, but as a religious rite. (See Acts, chapters 10, 11, and 15.) However, the epistles make it clear that all religious significance of circumcision was done away with in Christ (Galatians 5:6; Colossians 2:11).

Discussing This Subject with Your Children

Occasionally the question of circumcision comes up when a preschooler notices some boys' penises look a bit different than others. The question can be handled honestly and matter-of-factly in a manner similar to the illustration about little Jeff and the museum statue in chapter three.

Elementary school children and junior highs may wonder about what kind of "loose skin" is taken off in circumcision. Showing them the pictures illustrating circumcision (Figure 17) may help answer their questions. Or you might describe it like this: Picture someone who had a sweater sleeve that extended beyond the hand. If the person wanted to wash the hand, he could pull the sweater back; *or* he could have the sweater sleeve shortened so that the hand would be exposed. Circumcision is like having the sweater sleeve shortened so that it is easier to keep the head (glans) of the penis clean.

Teen-agers should be aware of the *smegma* (a substance secreted by the glands just under the head of the penis) that may accumulate, giving off a bad odor and causing irritation. This should be cleaned away regularly whether or not the boy has been circumcised. A boy whose penis has not been circumcised should make sure he pushes back the foreskin far enough to be certain the entire head of the penis is washed thoroughly.

160

Crush

A crush is a deep infatuation for another person, an emotional involvement that may be very intense at the time but which is of short duration. A young person feels a great attraction for somebody who may be of the same or the opposite sex. Often that person is quite out of reach and hasn't the slightest idea he or she is being admired. But the person who has the "crush," daydreams about the other person, watches for that person in a crowd, admires and sometimes tries to imitate various characteristics of the "hero," and looks upon that person as being virtually perfect. (It differs from mature love which can recognize and accept faults, among other things.)

A young person may have a crush on a television personality, sports hero, Scout leader, school teacher, or on a very special friend. Crushes are normal and are part of growing up. They help a young person develop emotionally, and prepare him for the kind of love that can lead to marriage and family living. Actually, a crush merely means that certain qualities in someone are being admired which gives rise to an exaggerated feeling of fondness and emotional attachment.

Your Children and Crushes

Parents need to be understanding and sympathetic about crushes. Quite likely they can remember such feelings from their own youth. In fact, "hero worship" can be good if the person admired possesses the qualities that children would do well to develop in their own lives. What social scientists speak of as "role models" are important in growing up. Children like to "be like" and "be with" persons they admire. If their "heroes" can be outstanding Christians (camp counselors, Christian athletes or musicians), there can be a great influence for good. Paul told the Corinthians to be imitators of him, as he was of Christ (1 Corinthians 11:1).

A word of caution is sometimes in order for teen-agers who may take the crush too seriously and act in inappropriate ways. Occasionally a teen-age girl may have a crush on one of her high school teachers, even though he is a much older married man. Rather than recognize what she feels is a deep admiration for certain *qualities* and not a total affection for the man as a complete person (she doesn't even know him well), the girl may believe she has been overtaken by a strange romantic passion beyond her control. Imagining she is "in love," she may write him a note describing her feelings. Obviously, this is unwise and embarrassing for the teacher. A parent at this point must show deep empathy, consideration and understanding and help such young persons think through their feelings.

Exhibitionism

Exhibitionism is an abnormal desire to publicly expose one's genitals to strangers. Sometimes referred to as "indecent exposure," it is considered to be the most common of all sexual offenses, and there is great variation from one state to another with regard to laws and penalties.[12] Most exhibitionists are men, who are usually harmless. That is, they have no intention of hurting or even touching those to whom they expose themselves.

Sometimes a quiet family man, a citizen known and respected in his community, may become an exhibitionist to the great shock of all who know him. There are cases where such a man is overtaken with a strange compulsion to display his erect penis to women in a shopping center, subway station, or in a hospital waiting room. Psychiatrists point out that exhibitionists may come from all social classes and all walks of life. But there are indications that they all have one thing in common—"a relative lack of masculine self-esteem."[13] They seem to have deep feelings of inferiority and low self-confidence. At

162

the same time they have ambivalent feelings toward women. On the one hand, they fear women; on the other, they sense feelings of dependency upon them.

Most exhibitionists began doing it during their teen-age years and repeat the act until caught. They often feel a deep sense of shame and actually seek arrest as a way of "atonement." Most, however, do not seek psychiatric help unless urged to do so by their families or legal authorities. Exhibitionism is considered to be a form of personality disorder, and it is only under extreme stress that many such men display themselves. Rarely do exhibitionists go on to do other sexual crimes (such as rape), though understandably their act often frightens persons into thinking that this is their intent.

Discussing This Subject with Your Children

Very small children can be taught the importance of modesty. Without conveying a sense of shame, parents can help their youngsters understand there are certain things one does not do in public. Like taking off one's clothes, handling one's sexual organs, or urinating in public view. Little children often do such things quite innocently and parents should not be unduly harsh. At the same time, parents can help children understand part of growing up is recognizing some things are private, personal matters.

Children with such attitudes will be aware that an act of public exhibitionism by an adult is strange and frightening. It can be explained that such persons are "sick in their minds" and don't really understand what they are doing. Should the children ever happen to see such a person, they should never look, talk, or accept an invitation to go with him. Rather, they should immediately walk away and talk the incident over with their parents. If parents understand, accept, and do not over-react with shock, disgust and terror, the children are not likely to be adversely affected by what they have seen. The less the incident is emphasized the better. Children will soon forget it.

While some exhibitionists display themselves to children, there seem to be more who are seeking to evoke responses of surprise, shock, and horror from adolescent girls and adult women. Teen-age girls should be aware of this and should understand this to be a form of mental illness. The fact, however, that most exhibitionists are not likely to progress to an actual sexual act should *not* be interpreted to mean there is never any danger or that caution should be thrown to the winds. Youngsters of all ages should know enough about sex crimes to steer clear of perilous situations. *Balance* is needed in this teaching task of parents, because realistic warnings need to be sounded at the same time that we take care not to arouse unwarranted fears and suspicions in the minds of children.

Fornication

When an unmarried person engages in sexual intercourse, the act is called *fornication*. The Bible repeatedly makes clear that fornication, like adultery, is a sin against God (Mark 7:21; 1 Corinthians 6:13-20; Galatians 5:19 ff.; Ephesians 5:3 ff.; 1 Thessalonians 4:1-8; Hebrews 13:4; Revelation 2:20). In the New Testament, the Greek word *porneia* is traditionally translated "fornication." In many newer translations it appears as "immorality." The word refers to sexual intercourse with prostitutes (particularly temple prostitutes) and sexual intercourse with a variety of partners (promiscuity). It also is used sometimes in reference to *any* sexual act between two persons not married to each other, including instances that technically might be considered acts of adultery. (See Matthew 5:32; 19:9; 1 Corinthians 5:1.)

But what if a man and woman are in love with each

164

other, maybe even engaged? If they desire sex relations before their wedding, would their act also be fornication? Some "new morality" advocates say no—that fornication only refers to acts of promiscuity or acts in which another person is being used as a thing and exploited selfishly for one's own gratification. They maintain that the "old morality" concentrated only on the act, whereas a "new morality" looks on the specific situation and motivation of the persons concerned. This is called situation ethics.

However, the noted classical scholar E. M. Blaiklock points out that no such distinctions were in the minds of the New Testament writers. Rather, they included under the meaning of porneia "all sex-experience outside the one legitimate occasion—marriage. . . . There is not a phrase or word in the New Testament which in any way condones extra-marital sex. . . . The whole force of the New Testament is behind chastity and the sanctity of marriage."[4] There is no indication that "love makes it all right." Indeed, Paul told the Corinthians that if sex desire in courtship became too great, the lovers should marry. Otherwise they might fall into the sin of fornication (1 Corinthians 7:9,36).

Sex before marriage is an attempt to experience a *physical* union without the *total* one flesh commitment marriage involves. The Bible teaches that this is wrong. First because the marital union is much more than sex. It is the merging of two lives into a permanent publicly declared, one-flesh relationship. And second, sex before marriage easily becomes the main focus of a couple's relationship, impairing the spiritual growth of two people. Premarital sex becomes the be-all-end-all of dating life. Many couples claim when they're together they get so wrapped up in the novelty of sex they don't even know how to talk or really get to know each other.

In such an atmosphere, sex often becomes an "idol"

and draws people away from God rather than toward Him. There is also a danger of promiscuity in premarital sex, even when the intention is to have sex only with the person one happens to love at the time. Since there is no permanent commitment, there is a real possibility that one or the other might have a change of heart. Not only is ending a relationship more painful when there has been sexual intimacy, but most often the individuals move on to other partners and report the same life style. This is nothing short of promiscuity (sex with a variety of different partners)—even though it is limited to one at a time. Sometimes this is called "serial promiscuity."[15]

Discussing This Subject with Your Children

Preschoolers, in their limited understanding of sex, tend to think of it only in terms of having babies. They are unlikely to wonder or ask about anything pertaining to fornication.

However, by the time a child reaches school age, he is beginning to hear pieces of information that puzzle him. Perhaps he hears sex remarks and jokes from friends who have older siblings. Perhaps he hears about an "unwed mother" and wonders how this can be. He can be told that it *is* possible to have babies without being married, but that this isn't what God wants. And persons who have sex before marriage aren't acting in a way that pleases Him. God planned that babies should be born into loving families where there will be a mother and father to care for them and guide them in their growing-up years.

Older elementary school children can learn that it isn't just to avoid premarital pregnancy that sexual intercourse before marriage is displeasing to God. A fifth-grader came home and told his mother that the boys at school had teased him because they were talking about "making bases" with a girl and he didn't understand what they were talking about. "Boy, are you dumb!" they said and then explained the step-by-step process of increasing sexual involvement. The boy's mother was able to help him to see that this attitude was an incorrect way to think about girls. That this was treating girls as though they were just *things*, not people. It was like saying girls were just something to conquer, rather than being friends and companions with them. It was thinking of a girl's body only, and not about her mind and personality. These are some of the reasons such behavior is considered to be sin in God's sight.

With teen-agers, the issue becomes more crucial. They're aware of all the talk about sex in the mass media and the arguments used to justify premarital permissiveness. If parents can be understanding and hear them out, teens will be much more ready to hear what parents have to say, and more important, what *God* has to say. Why not explore and discuss related Scriptures during family devotions?

Homosexuality

Homosexuality refers to the act of engaging in sexual relations with a person of one's own sex. Once considered to be the most unmentionable of all sexual practices, it is now openly and freely discussed. Because of this, parents should be aware of the meaning of various terms related to the topic.

Experts in many fields (such as psychology and psychiatry, sociology, anthropology, medicine, law and others) are at present conducting research to come to a greater understanding of this subject. There has even been confusion with regard to a definition. Realizing there *must* be a clear and workable definition of homosexuality in order for reliable scientific research to be carried out, Dr. Paul Gebhard, director of the Institute for Sex Research at Indiana University, has written:

"We have found the most practical definition of homosexual behavior to be: physical contact between two individuals of the same gender which both recognize as being sexual in nature and which ordinarily results in sexual arousal. Psychological homosexual response may be defined as the desire for such physical contact and/or conscious sexual arousal from thinking of or seeing persons of the same gender."[16]

The word *homosexual* literally means "pertaining to the same sex." It comes from the Greek word *homos,* meaning "one and the same," *not* from the Latin word *homo* which means "man, human being." The term refers to both men and women, although female homosexuality is called *lesbianism.* The name derives from the ancient Greek island of Lesbos, where an educated woman named Sappho conducted a school for girls and is reputed to have "fallen in love" with some of her students and to have addressed sensuous poems to them. Rumors circulated that the women of the island engaged in sex relations with one another.

Present-day homosexual persons refer to themselves as "gay"—a word which contradicts the prevalent idea that homosexual persons are unhappy, depressed, or emotionally maladjusted. Many, in the "gay liberation movement," want society to recognize homosexuality as a legitimate way of life for those who wish it. They do not feel homosexuality is an illness, and they don't wish to be "cured." Organized gay life consists of a special "community of understanding" in which persons engaging in homosexual practices know of one another, get together in special "gay bars" or other meeting places, and organize their social life and living patterns around their sexual interest.

Derogatory slang terms sometimes used in reference to homosexual persons are queer, fag, fruit, pansy, drag queen (referring to a man who acts and dresses in imitation of a woman), and butch or dyke (referring to a woman who plays the part of a man).

The word *heterosexual* means "pertaining to the opposite sex" and refers to persons whose sexual interest is directed toward the opposite sex and not toward their own. Men are attracted toward women; women are attracted toward men. They marry and have children. This is heterosexuality. The word comes from the Greek *heteros* which means "the other of two." The gay community speaks of heterosexual persons as persons who are straight.

Another term to keep in mind is *bisexual*. It comes from the Latin word *bis,* meaning "twice," and refers to persons who have sexual relations with *either* sex. A bisexual individual, whether male or female, engages in sex relations with both men and women. Some such persons speak of it as "swinging both ways" or "operating on AC and DC."

A persistent myth about homosexual persons is that they somehow look different from heterosexual individuals. But many homosexual men are rugged, masculine types and not at all the stereotype of a "sissified, effeminate male." And many lesbian women are extremely feminine and not at all mannish in looks or behavior. Conversely, many girls and women are "tomboy" types but there is nothing in the least homosexual about them. And many men are quiet, artistic, introspective, poetic and gentle and yet have no inclination toward homosexual behavior whatsoever. Christians especially must be cautious about stereotyping and judging people.

There are two categories of homosexuality. The first, *career homosexuality,* is sometimes called "hard-core homosexuality." This refers to persons who habitually practice homosexuality over a long period of time. The second is called *situational homosexuality*. This refers to people who are *not* committed to a life of homosexual

169

activity. They might be early teen-agers who, out of curiosity, masturbate together. Or they might be persons who engaged in homosexual acts in unusual circumstances, like a boarding school, prison, or in the military. Once the unusual circumstances have been removed, the person may again prefer the company of the opposite sex.

Although much research is being directed toward the study of homosexuality, the subject is not yet well understood. Some try to explain it from a *medical* standpoint, though at present there is no final proof that it is something innate and caused by a hormone imbalance." Others consider it to be an illness. Some believe people are "born homosexual" but the evidence is extremely weak. *Psychological* explanations view homosexuality as the result of certain childhood experiences, such as a dominant mother. Or as a sign of arrested psychological development in which a person purportedly remains at an earlier stage of interest in his own sex rather than progressing toward interest in the opposite sex as a sign of maturity.

Sociological explanations suggest that homosexuality may be a learned experience. All persons have sexual desires, but heterosexuality or homosexuality depends upon where they learn to direct those desires. In the case of the homosexual persons, it may be that they were introduced to sexual acts with persons of their own sex during adolescence. This may have resulted because they did not know how to relate and form friendships with persons of the opposite sex. After having engaged in acts of homosexuality, persons may feel they must *be* homosexual by nature. If they are labeled homosexual by others, they begin living according to the "label" society gives them, whereupon society says, "Aha! We told you so. That person is gay." Sociologists call this a "self-fulfilling prophecy."

Questions sometimes arise about the types of behavior

170

in which homosexual persons engage. Many of their sex acts may be compared to heterosexual petting and the foreplay that precedes intercourse. Lesbians fondle, caress and kiss in the manner of husbands and wives, and practice mutual masturbation, focusing on the clitoris. Some may imitate heterosexual intercourse through genital apposition, i.e., the genitals of one rubbing against those of the other. Lesbians also practice oral-genital contact—the type known as *cunnilingus*, in which the mouth is placed over the partner's vulva. Occasionally some women in a homosexual relationship use fingers or an artificial penis to be inserted into the vagina.

When males engage in homosexual practices, they also use the techniques of mutual masturbation and oral-genital contact—the type known as *fellatio*, in which the mouth receives the partner's penis. Much less common is the practice of anal intercourse in which the anus is used as a substitute vagina.[18] Technically, the term "sodomy" refers to the act of anal intercourse.

It should be emphasized that no sexual act in itself can be called "homosexual." A sex technique becomes a homosexual practice only when it is engaged in by two persons of the same sex. If a husband kisses his wife's breast, obviously he is not engaging in homosexuality. But if a woman fondles and kisses another woman's breast, the act becomes homosexual. This is mentioned because there are some married couples who fear that any marital sexual practice beyond the insertion of the penis into the vagina is somehow a "perversion."

As we endeavor to come to an understanding of homosexuality in the light of the Bible, it is helpful to think of three broad, general categories of human relationships.

First, there is the relationship of marriage as described by Christ in Matthew 19:4-6. In the beginning God created human beings as male and female. He then arranged the institution of marriage so they could become

171

one flesh, a uniting of mind, spirit and body. Using the symbols for male and female, we might diagram it in the following manner:

One Flesh Relationship

$$\male + \female = \text{(overlapping)}$$

Male   Female   One Flesh

Second, there is the deep relationship of a close friend. It's best illustrated in the story of David and Jonathan (see 1 Samuel 18:1-4; 20:17,23,40-42; 2 Samuel 1:26). The Bible tells us that each loved the other "as his own soul." Because of this they made a covenant with one another, pledging to be friends always, and acknowledging the Lord's presence in their relationship, asking Him to be between them always (1 Samuel 20:23,42). When they parted, they wept as they embraced and kissed one another. Yet there is absolutely no hint of homosexuality in their relationship. It was not a "one flesh" relationship, but rather a relationship of "one soul." The Bible gives us other examples of such friendships in Paul and Timothy, and Ruth and Naomi. We might also think of John, the beloved disciple who leaned against Jesus at the Last Supper. Or the close friendship Jesus had with Mary, Martha, and Lazarus, or with Mary Magdalene. One-soul relationships may exist between two men, two women, or a man and a woman. They involve a union of mind, heart and spirit—but *not* a physical union (which is reserved for the one-flesh relationship). Thus we have:

One Soul Relationship

Moving on to a third area, we come to the matter of homosexual practices as they are treated in the Bible. Passages which deal with this are Romans 1:26,27; 1 Corinthians 6:9; 1 Timothy 1:10; Genesis 19:1-11; Leviticus 18:22; 20:13; and Judges 19:22-30. Passages in Deuteronomy 23:17,18; 1 Kings 14:24; 15:12; 2 Kings 23:7, refer to the male cult prostitutes of the fertility religions—although some Bible scholars express doubt that the cultic sexual acts were necessarily homosexual.[19]

It should be noticed that when the Bible speaks of the wrongness of homosexual practices, the context is often connected with a warning against idolatry and the customs of heathen nations surrounding the people of Israel. It also should be noticed that persons who engaged in homosexual practices are not beyond God's grace, or that their sins are somehow worse than other kinds of sins.

If Romans 1:26,27 is read in the context of the verses following, we see that envy, gossip and disobedience to parents are but a few of the sins that are just as great a violation of God's will. There is no basis or place for smug, self-righteous pride that some Christians show as they judge and condemn those with problems of homosexuality. In Corinth, many such persons turned to the Saviour and experienced a new life in Christ (1 Corinthians 6:9-11).

We must also keep in mind the scriptural emphasis is always on homosexual acts or practices, and *not* on a "homosexual nature" or orientation. Bisexuality was common in the ancient world; persons who engaged in homosexual acts usually had sex relations with persons of the opposite sex also. It was only in the late seventeenth century the idea grew up that some persons were "homosexual," that they had a nature different from others and that their condition was "a broad social role rather than . . . a sexual act."[20]

If we were to diagram the third category of relationships, we might have this:

One Sex (Sexual) Relationships

In such relationships, there is an attempt to *imitate* the one-flesh relationship that Jesus spoke of as being designed from the beginning by God for male and female. In many homosexual liaisons, the emphasis is on the physical aspect only, which then becomes lust and promiscuity. In other such relationships, there is a desire to imitate the one-flesh relationship in a fuller sense, in essence adding a physical dimension to the one-soul friendship relationship. This is sometimes called a homosexual marriage, and some couples of the same sex go through a ceremony (not legal at this writing) as a public declaration of their intent to form a permanent love relationship. The Scriptures do not speak about such a situation, but it would seem (from Matthew 19 and other passages) that this is not God's ideal according to His plan for marriage from the beginning of creation.

This Subject and Your Children

There is little likelihood that preschoolers will have questions about homosexuality. And there is no reason to stir up suspicions and fears about same-sex friendships and displays of affection as though these were somehow wrong. Occasionally, however, a question might come up about why two men or two women can't get married to each other; and parents may simply reply that God didn't plan it that way. He designed the bodies of men and women differently so that they could marry and have children.

174

Both younger children and elementary school children should have some awareness of homosexual seduction and child molestation. Certainly not all persons who engage in homosexual acts are interested in approaching children, but sometimes this is the case. Children should know never to accept gifts or offers of rides and the like when they are offered by strangers. And they should never let strangers of either sex (or acquaintances, for that matter) touch or examine their bodies, especially the genital area. One young boy was watching a movie at a neighborhood theater when a man moved up beside him and pretended he was a friend of the boy's father (this is a favorite trick of child molesters and children should be aware of it). The man kept suggesting the boy accompany him to the men's room (which the boy refused to do). Then he tried to unzip the boy's trousers. The child was wise enough to move away, and the man was later apprehended by the police.

In *any* case involving child-seduction or molestation, it is extremely important for parents to remain calm and reassuring to their youngsters. Often the emotional harm caused by panicky parents and other adults can be more serious than the original incident. The less the child is involved in legal procedures connected with the suspect's arrest, the better it will be for the child's emotional well-being.[21]

Grade-school children have some knowledge of homosexual activity through hearsay and slang terms. They may even ask how homosexual persons have sex relations with one another. Parents may reply that they go to bed together and kiss and caress like husbands and wives. Mature pre-teen-agers and adolescents may be given further information.

Many teen-agers (especially boys) worry about homosexuality, fearing such tendencies are present in themselves. Because there are so many fears, feelings of revulsion, and misconceptions about the subject, parents often aggravate the problem rather than help the young person. All too often, Christians seem to suspect homosexuality in any deep same-sex friendship. They confuse the two categories of one-soul and one-sex (sexual)—something the Bible never does. The noted Christian writer, C. S. Lewis, pointed out that persons who view all warm friendships as being inherently homosexual in nature are really telling us a great deal about themselves, namely that they don't understand what friendship really is and have never had a friend.[22]

It is perfectly normal for young adolescents to have "best friend" relationships with persons of the same sex. In fact, it's an important part of growing up and learning to get along with others. It can even be helpful in preparing for one's later marriage, because it provides the experience of a sharing-caring relationship with someone who has common interests and a similar outlook on life. The issue is sometimes confused in young people's minds because they have heard or read definitions of homosexuality that speak of it as "feelings of love or affection for someone of one's own sex." With such a definition in mind, Christians can become afraid of fulfilling the second great commandment—to love one's neighbor as oneself! It is well to remind ourselves that the Bible speaks only of homosexual *acts.* If a young person is fond of someone and enjoys his or her friend's company and never engages in homosexual *practices,* there is certainly no reason to think of the relationship as homosexual. Of course, no friendship should be allowed to be so exclusive that all others are cut out. Nor should friends ever act possessive, jealous and desirous of dominating one another.

Many behavioral scientists today believe the concept of "latent homosexuality" is misleading and useless.[23] They point out that *any*one could, under certain circumstances, engage in homosexual acts, just as we have the potential for many other undesirable acts. Yet we don't speak of ourselves as latent thieves or latent adulterers. Because someone has a fleeting homosexual thought or homosexual dream does not mean he has a basic hidden "homosexual nature." Some young teen-agers may have participated in a single episode of homosexual behavior out of curiosity and a sense of experimentation. This usually brings feelings of horror and shame afterwards, but it by no means indicates the young person will turn to homosexuality in adulthood. The situation may be different, however, where someone consciously and habitually fantasizes about engaging in homosexual acts.

Sex-role stereotypes should also not be permitted to cause teens to fear they are homosexually inclined. Wrong ideas should not be read into a girl's interest in athletics or engineering, or a boy's interest in writing poetry or playing a violin in preference to sports. People today are increasingly being encouraged to be themselves and not feel bound by roles imposed by society.

One family-life counselor suggests one of the greatest reasons for the development of homosexual patterns is a failure to learn to relate well to the opposite sex. Faulty relations with one's own sex may also be a factor. He suggests that parents encourage their youngsters in developing socially, especially during the early teens when so often parental teasing can discourage sensitive young persons in their budding heterosexuality.[24] Young persons feel clumsy and unsure of themselves in their early dating experiences and should not be made fun of. This same counselor emphasizes the importance of parental understanding of homosexuality and of adolescent fears about it. He urges parents to bring up the subject (taking advantage of mass media reports, for example, to open the conversation), since many teen-agers have questions and uncertainties related to the subject but hesitate to voice them unless encouraged to do so.

Marriage

Marriage may be defined as the legally sanctioned union of a man and a woman. It includes the sexual sharing of one another's bodies (1 Corinthians 7:3,4), economic interdependence, the privilege of bringing children into the world, and a public declaration indicating that a man and woman have thus committed themselves to one another and that a new social unit has been formed.

The pattern for marriage described in Genesis 2:24; Ephesians 5:31 and by Christ in Matthew 19:5, shows a "leave—cleave—become one flesh" pattern. This indicates that one family is left (father and mother), and a new family unit is formed (with one's spouse). This is not a matter between two individuals only, but involves society as a whole. In all cultures and in all times, marriage has been a public—not a private—matter. The forms of declaring it have varied widely. For example, there is no record of Isaac and Rebekah's having spoken wedding vows (Genesis 24:67); yet they fulfilled all the public declaration customs of their society, consisting mainly of an agreement between the respective families and the exchange of gifts, followed by an establishment of residence together as husband and wife (Genesis 24:1-67). Wedding customs during the times of the prophets, and later in New Testament times, included many other ceremonies and festivities. The particular forms are not important. What matters is that both the couple and their society recognize that a man and woman have entered a new status.

There are new responsibilities and obligations toward one another, toward society as a whole and any children they might bring into the world. The wedding ceremony in the *Book of Common Prayer* (1892 edition) speaks of marriage as an "honourable and holy estate" that should not be entered into "unadvisedly or lightly; but reverently, discreetly, advisedly, soberly, and in the fear of God." Marriage therefore becomes a serious matter.

Couples who feel they should have the privilege of living together without the state's permission granted on a piece of paper called a marriage license, fail to realize the reasons for legitimation of marriage. True, it is not the slip of paper or the words of the minister or justice of the peace that magically transform two singles into a married pair. It is their love and commitment to one another that makes them married. But public vows are a declaration to the world of that love and commitment. It means these two persons belong to each other alone. This in itself is an important reason for a public declaration of permanent commitment. Otherwise, other persons can be misled. (See Genesis 12:10-20; 20:1-18; and 26:6-11.) Other reasons for laws and regulations about marriage include the protection of the partners with regard to fairness in property, inheritance regulations, and protection of children. Couples should be legally married so their children can be guaranteed a legitimate status as well as having the physical and emotional care they need for a normal development.

This Subject and Your Children

This book has stressed that children of all ages can learn what God's plan for marriage is by observation and direct instruction. Children are never too young to learn. Even tiny preschoolers can grasp the warmth and beauty of the love a husband and wife have for each other. Marriage is a wonderful relationship—so wonderful the Scriptures repeatedly use it as an illustration of God's relationship to His people. But it is also a serious relationship; a fact that children should realize early.

179

With current rebellion against "the establishment," and concern for individual rights, many young people are questioning marriage as an institution regulated by society. Hopefully, the material provided and the arguments presented may be helpful in discussing the "why" of marriage both from a biblical and a sociological viewpoint.[25]

Masturbation

Masturbation is the act of stimulating one's own genitals, usually to the point of sexual climax (orgasm). Another name for it is *autoeroticism*. It is the experiencing of sexual pleasure alone, by oneself, without a partner. In males, the usual method of masturbation is to clasp the erect penis in the hand and to manipulate it vigorously in a jerking, up and down motion. Boys sometimes use the slang expression "jerking" or "jacking off" in reference to masturbation. In females, masturbation usually involves stroking and rubbing the vulva area, with special concentration on the clitoris.

Only in recent years have various authorities begun taking a new look at the age-old fears, prejudices and myths of masturbation. Among those who are re-examining the subject in the light of the latest research are many evangelicals who have done a great deal of writing on the subject of sex.[26] There is still wide variation in the opinions of Christians with regard to masturbation, but an increasing number seem less willing to label it *sin*. Many in fact encourage the practice as being far more desirable for young people in a sex-saturated society than the practice of premarital intercourse or intimate petting as means of sexual release.

In the past, masturbation was looked upon as vile, loathsome and physically, psychologically, and spiritually harmful. It was referred to as "self-abuse," "self-pollution," "playing with yourself," and "the solitary vice."

180

Medical doctors, clergymen and educators warned parents about the dire consequences that would occur if their children masturbated. Masturbation was said to "use up the vital forces," cause insanity, deafness, blindness, epilepsy, baldness, weight loss, and weakness. It was also said to cause brain damage, weak eyes, blunting of the senses of taste and smell, and also impair their nervous system. In males, masturbation supposedly used up the supply of semen and caused sterility and impotence. In females, it was thought masturbation somehow damaged child-bearing capability. The idea that masturbation caused teen-age acne was also added to the list, as was Freud's notion that women who had masturbated would have difficulty achieving sexual response in marriage.

Believing these myths (all of which are scientifically untrue and have been proven to have no basis in fact), parents went to incredible ends to "preserve" their innocent children from this "wicked, harmful vice." Some parents beat their children if caught in the act and warned them they would be sent to hell because of it. They purchased special chastity belts for boys (patented in this present century), or aluminum mitts in which children's hands were locked at bedtime. Handcuffs also were sometimes used. Someone even came up with an idea for a device that could be attached to a boy's bed-covers and which would ring a buzzer in the father's bedroom if the boy had an erection, whereupon the father could rush to "save the boy from himself"! Even such extremes as surgery and other physical means were used when shaming, scolding, and mechanical devices failed. Physicians would cut out a girl's clitoris or suture the labia in an effort to stop masturbation.[27] Operations were also performed on boys "to render the act physically impossible." One medical writer and lecturer suggested in a 1917 publication[28] the "repeated blistering" of the penis

181

as another treatment if other means failed. One particular "surgical treatment" this same writer recommended in extreme cases was a bizarre practice known in Roman times as *infibulation.* The prepuce would be drawn over the glans of the penis, and a ring placed through the foreskin, "locking" it into place! Another distinguished physician is reputed to have even commended a father for "curing" his son of masturbation by means of castration![29] There is no doubt about it; attitudes toward masturbation make up an embarrassing page in the history of medical science.

Now, however, it is recognized that masturbation is not physiologically harmful. Some books warn against carrying it "to excess," but excess is never defined. Other authorities point out that the body reaches its own satiation point, physical exhaustion in a female and inability to maintain an erection in a male. Thus, physiologically speaking it wouldn't be possible to reach a point of excess. The body would simply stop responding as occurs in cases of repeated intercourse during a very short interval of time.

Masturbation *can* be a problem and the matter of excess very real in the case of a person using masturbatory activity as a means of escape from things that torment him. A person who finds masturbating compulsive and uses it to flee from frustration, loneliness, or a poor self-image needs counseling. The problem isn't the masturbation, but what lies behind it. Incidentally, many people who are aware of what seems to be a preoccupation with masturbatory activity among the mentally ill wonder if perhaps masturbation hasn't caused the mental illness. But such isn't the case. It's just that many mental patients tend to be totally uninhibited and make no distinctions between public and private behavior. Thus, they often tend to fondle the sex organs in public.

Moving into still another area, and viewing the subject

in the context of one's spiritual life, the Christian may want to think about the warnings about "excess" from another angle: Wouldn't "sexual excess" in *any* form be that which becomes idolatrous and draws our focus away from God, or that which causes us to become self-centered and unconcerned about others? These are the kinds of questions the Christian must ask.

Many sex educators are convinced the only possible harm that comes from masturbation is the guilt many young people carry because of this. Much of this burden could be lifted if parents and teen-agers understood the subject better and could rid themselves of the fears and myths. If, of course, there is a reason for guilt because of sexual sins in the thought life, as Christ warned about in Matthew 5:28, then the message of Christ's forgiveness and healing should be emphasized.

One school of thought has in the past spoken of masturbation as "immature behavior," a holdover from the self-centeredness of early childhood. But this too is being questioned and discarded today. Some marriage counselors counsel wives troubled with lack of sexual response to practice masturbation in an effort to become acquainted with their bodies' capabilities for erotic pleasure. It is recommended they communicate to their husbands what is most pleasing.

Masturbation is sometimes recommended by physicians and counselors as a means of sexual release for husbands whose wives are ill or when they are separated for long periods of time. Masturbation is suggested as a means of release from sexual tensions in the case of widows and widowers who are suddenly cut off from an active sex life. The reasoning is that this is far better than acts of promiscuity, adultery, and fornication.

And, say some, should not this same reasoning apply in cases of the never married, yet who have just as real

183

sexual needs as anyone else? Also, what about teen-agers? They are at an age in which all the newly awak-ened sexual drives and feelings are surging through their bodies and filling their minds with thoughts and ques-tions. Yet they're not ready for marriage in such a com-plex society as ours. Might not masturbation be the one acceptable outlet available to them so that sex energies can be drained off without harm to themselves or others? Others go even further and speak of masturbation as a necessary and helpful part of sexual development which will have positive and beneficial value in marriage.

These then are some of today's prevailing views. As a parent, you might be confused at this point, especially as you think back to your own youth and remember how you felt about the subject. Many if not most Christian fa-thers, for example, can remember the intense struggles they had during their teens and the agony of the guilt they experienced because of masturbation. What now should they tell their sons? That it's OK—to just go ahead with the practice? Or should they hold on to the old views that reinforced their own guilt?

This is one of those grey areas in which the Bible is si-lent and in which each Christian is going to have to be persuaded in his own mind. It may well be one of those matters that could be included under "Christian liberty" or "things indifferent." Behavior that may be sinful for one person in this area may not be so for another. Admit-tedly, it would be easier for all of us if we could just say, as we can about adultery or fornication, that "masturba-tion is sinful." Or "masturbation is permissible." It just isn't clear-cut. Thus, parents should be thoroughly familiar with the subject in making up their own minds.

Christian authors seem to vary widely in their views on masturbation. There seems to be a continuum of opinions ranging from "masturbation is sin in God's sight" to "mas-turbation is a gift of God." Secular authorities speak of a

184

fourfold division of masturbation attitudes,[30] and among Christian writers similar categories emerge. As a parent, you should have some idea of each of these, not only to help you come to a position of your own, but, also, that you'll be aware of the opinions expressed in books your young people are reading.

First, there is the view that masturbation is sin, a misuse of a good gift of God which is displeasing in His sight. Most older Christian books clearly took this as a firm position,[31] viewing masturbation as "fleshly lust."

A second category of Christian authors look upon masturbation as being wrong for a Christian because it is less than the *ideal* standard God intends for sex. God's ideal is two persons in communion with one another coming together in one flesh as husband and wife. They feel the wrongness of masturbation lies in using something in solitude that was meant for partnership.[32]

There is a third category of Christians who look upon masturbation as a matter that is morally neutral, a matter of Christian liberty to be decided between the individual's conscience and the Lord. Such persons are open to new physiological and psychological insights, yet are not ready to commit themselves to the position that masturbation is a *necessary* part of sexual development for teen-agers. Nor, on the other hand, are they prepared to say that masturbation is sinful. They don't wish to pass judgment on others and tend to feel that each person should make up his own mind. They are more concerned with how sex is used and misused *in relationships with other persons;* thus their books often don't discuss masturbation at all.[33]

In a fourth category are those Christians who suggest that masturbation may be a legitimate way of releasing sexual tensions. Miles, for example, advocates a "limited program of masturbation for the purpose of self-control."[34]

185

He reasons that a young man before marriage or a married man whose wife is ill or separated from him for a period of time continues to produce and store semen. If this is not released through a nocturnal emission, he may feel uncomfortable. Yet he does not want to sin against God by indulging in premarital or extramarital sexual intercourse. Might not masturbation be a God-given way out? Miles suggests that it is. However, he seems to hold a double standard, saying that masturbation for the sake of self-control, not lust, is right for boys but wrong for girls. He believes females have no *physical* reason to seek release. This, however, is questionable in view of the Masters/Johnson findings that in some women the lack of sexual release may actually bring about physical distress in the form of chronic pelvic vascular congestion.[35]

The psychiatrist, M. O. Vincent, also suggests that masturbation may be a legitimate means of releasing sexual tensions for a Christian—male or female.[36] He suggests that "if masturbation is utilized to decrease lust or excessive sexual fantasies, it is good."[37]

Closely related to this category of Christian thinking is the position that masturbation is "a gift of God" which can be beneficial to a young person's overall development. Thus, Charlie Shedd in *The Stork Is Dead* speaks of masturbation as "the wise provision of a very wise Creator." Something God gave us "because He knew we'd need it!"[38] He points out that in a sex-saturated society, there needs to be some means of release. He suggests masturbation is preferable to teen-age intercourse. Hettlinger is another author who believes that masturbation can be viewed as a gift of God.[39]

If there is such variance among Christians toward masturbation, what conclusions should Christian parents draw as they try to guide their children? First, recognize that sincere and devoted Christians have differences of opinion with regard to this subject as well as others—

abortion, for example. The five major viewpoints have been presented here to acquaint you with all of them and to give you some basis for drawing your own conclusions. Take time to consider each of them.

Next, keep in mind the Scriptures are silent on the subject. It used to be thought the "sin of Onan" mentioned in Genesis 38:8-10 was masturbation. That's why masturbation is sometimes called "onanism." It seemed like a good proof-text for parents to frighten their children, "God will strike you dead if you 'play with yourself'." Yet, Onan's sin was not masturbation. Rather, he failed to complete an act of sexual intercourse. Onan simply withdrew before emission of semen because he did not want to fulfill an Old Testament law which required the brother of a dead man to go to the man's widow and produce an heir in the name of the deceased brother. That was the sin for which he was punished. The wording of the *King James Version* in passages like Micah 2:1 and 1 Corinthians 6:9 was taken by some to refer to masturbation. But a careful look at the context, as well as the use of modern translations, makes it clear this subject is not being discussed at all. The Bible simply doesn't talk about masturbation.

How then can we know what to do about it? Perhaps it will be helpful to think back to the four functions of sex which were mentioned in chapter two: procreation, recreation, communication and release. We saw the Bible discuss all four aspects and indicate that sex in all its fulness (with all four areas present) can only be experienced in marriage. However, the Scriptures do not hide the fact that there is such a thing as sexual tension and a need for sex release. Paul said that "it is better to marry than to be aflame with passion" (1 Corinthians 7:9).

However, what if the possibility of marriage is not open? Also, would we want to encourage teen-agers,

187

who are encouraged not to marry as early as they did during Bible times, to jump into a marriage simply to have a legitimate way of draining off sex energies? We now must ask ourselves if masturbation might not be an option.

If sex is compartmentalized into the four areas mentioned, it might be possible for a Christian to look upon masturbation simply as *release*. It cannot, of course, be a substitute for sex in all its fulness as may be experienced in marriage. Nevertheless it is a helpful way to deal with sex tensions when other outlets are not possible. Viewed this way, one needn't feel guilty as one wouldn't feel guilty about a "wet dream." One writer questions the assumption that nocturnal emissions are the only means God intended for release of the male sex drive. He points out such dreams are almost always highly erotic and wonders why this is thought "better" for a Christian than masturbation where thoughts can be consciously controlled.[40]

This brings us to the matter of sex thoughts or fantasy. Sex researchers have found that about three-fourths of males and one-half of females experience erotic fantasies during masturbation.[41] Sometimes counselors suggest this is good because otherwise the act would be merely mechanical. However, it's only a matter of opinion and there is no proof or widespread agreement. But for the Christian, there is a different problem, because Jesus spoke of the error of committing sexual sins in the thought life. If a Christian young person engages in masturbation in such a way as to encourage lustful thoughts and to increase (rather than control) sexual desire, then the act becomes sin. On the other hand, if a young person accepts the position that masturbation may be a means of release and self-control, then he must come to terms with the kinds of thoughts he will allow himself to have. In view of Matthew 5:28, it would obviously be wrong to imagine having sex relations with an acquaintance while masturbating. One way to guard against wrong kinds of fantasy might be to concentrate one's thoughts on the beauty of sex in the context of marriage.

On the other hand, we need not conclude that masturbation (with or without fantasy) is the *only* way to deal with teen-age sex drives. While self-stimulation is a widespread practice the world over, we need not conclude that it is necessary and essential for normal human development. Some young people do not masturbate. This does not mean that they're unhealthy or abnormal or that they will be incapable of a satisfactory sex life in marriage. There are Christian young people who are alert to temptations associated with masturbation (particularly with regard to the kinds of thoughts that come to mind) who choose to steer clear of the whole sequence of events that researchers say so often leads to desires to masturbate—pornographic pictures and articles, certain types of movies and books, necking and petting, even unusually constricting clothing.

Christian teen-agers can know that God is very much aware of their struggles. They can know that God understands, cares and stands ready to help in their sex life just as much as in any other area of life.

The matter of sublimation should also be mentioned. This is the idea that sex energies can be drained off, burned up, or channeled into other activities. At one time, both Christian and secular books suggested this as the best way of dealing with sexual tensions. Now the idea has been discarded by many as being impractical, unrealistic and unworkable. Some believe such an approach encourages a denial of our sexuality and is repressive. However, there is a positive side that shouldn't be overlooked. Many Christian young people fill their active lives with sports, music and a variety of Christian services. As one focuses on a broad range of activities, plus the giving of oneself to others in acts of Christian empathy, concern and love, there is less likelihood of an *unhealthy* preoccupation with masturbation.

Perhaps a different look at the whole matter of "sex drives" is also needed. Dr. Lester Kirkendall suggests that perhaps too much emphasis has been put upon the biological side, so that most people think of teen-agers (boys, in particular) as "burning with sexual desire." That this is an inevitable "manifestation of the 'glands' and their vigorous functioning." He writes:

"The actual behavior and experiences of young men in their middle and late teens—and here I speak from an experience of over thirty-five years of direct work with them—suggests a different view. Some are 'burning.' They experience genuine difficulty in containing and directing their sexual desires. Others who are thoroughly healthy and in the best of physical condition do not experience 'burning' sexual desires. Their sexual behavior also indicates that they have little difficulty in adjusting to the sexual side of their nature."[42]

Professor Kirkendall goes on to express his belief that "the strength of the sex drive is determined largely by the way an individual thinks and feels toward sex." Persons for whom sexual tension becomes a bothersome problem may not be "pushed" and "driven" so much by *physiological* urges as they are by a *mental* state of unresolved conflicts and problems. Kirkendall reports his observation that teen-age boys and young men who have family problems, frustrations in getting along with people in general, or feelings of failure and lack of self-confidence tend to have strong, demanding sex drives. In contrast, "those individuals who felt their sex drives easily managed and caused them little or no difficulty often expressed feelings of satisfaction about themselves and their relations with others."[43] Yet, says Kirkendall, there is no reason to think that those in this second category are "weak in their sexual capacities" or less endowed sexually than those in the first group.

If it is true that a great deal of what is generally called "sex drive" is really dependent upon a state of mind, then much more emphasis needs to be directed toward creating *proper attitudes* toward sex. Kirkendall feels we must clarify our ideas about sex drive if we really care about the sex education of young people. The term as it is now used suggests something entirely physical and ignores the psychological factors which are actually more crucial in determining one's sexual conduct. Instead of using the expression "sex drive" as a catch-all phrase, we need to make distinctions between capacity, performance and desire.[44]

"We also need a clearer idea of the extent to which the *drive for expression through sex* (this is the way the phrase should be worded) is the result of physical conditions, and the extent to which it arises from the individual's psychological state or from social conditions."[45]

Kirkendall's comments seem to have some relevance to the subject at hand, since most people tend to think of masturbation only in relation to *physical urges* rather than taking into account these other factors.

This isn't meant to deny the real biological feelings that everybody experiences as part of sexual development. But seeing there are other elements involved, young people may be helped to realize the problem isn't too big, mysterious or overwhelming, that it can't be brought under control. God never intended that sex should control or use us; rather *we* are to use and control sex! And we can ask God to help us do this. Sex was meant to be a gift, not a slave driver.

This Subject and Your Children

Children are curious about everything, including their own bodies. Don't be surprised if even an infant explores the genital area of the body and seems to find such touching enjoyable. You needn't feel compelled to slap the tiny hand or move it away. Babies and toddlers are getting acquainted with their bodies and themselves.

It is however during the teen years that masturbation takes on a different meaning. Now it is no longer a matter of simple curiosity or childish pleasure, but takes on a deeper sexual meaning. Because so many new and different feelings and sensations arise with the onset of puberty, it's hard for a teen-ager to understand what is happening inside him. The body that has been "home" for more than a dozen years suddenly seems strange and different. New urges, moods and physical sensations seem to be bursting out all over. Using a hand to explore the familiar body which has now become so *un*familiar and novel, the young person stumbles upon unusual delights which both frighten and fascinate. There comes an awakening of wonder at the body's sexual capacities and capabilities. Then comes the thought: Aren't these feelings wrong? I wonder if anybody else feels like this? These new sensations scare me, yet it feels so good! How should I think about this? What should I do about these urges?

Parents can help by assuring their teen-agers that there is nothing "wrong." In fact, what is happening in their bodies is very wonderful! Parents should also realize that anxieties about masturbation are common among young people. Adolescents are deeply concerned about the subject and have many questions; yet it is one of the hardest areas for them to discuss. Who would understand? Parents are usually uneasy and shocked about the matter. Adults in general seem judgmental and full of negative reactions, conveniently forgetting their own youthful struggles (or is it that they are painfully remembering them?). And peers can't seem to help, because they're also uncertain about what is happening.

It may help parents and teen-agers to realize how common the practice of masturbation is. Statistical studies show that ninety percent of males over fifteen years of age have engaged in some form of masturbation that leads to orgasm. During early adolescence, the average frequency is from two to three times weekly. Among females, from fifty to sixty percent have masturbated to orgasm, but less often (usually only once or twice a month).[46] These statistics are not limited to teen-agers but include older and single people, widows, widowers, divorced persons and married persons. (For example, when a spouse is incapacitated or away, or in cases where one spouse desires sexual pleasure and release more frequently than the other and thus practices masturbation out of consideration for the partner, reasoning that autoeroticism is certainly to be preferred to going outside the marriage or forcing the spouse to conform to one's wishes.) They also include those who have only masturbated once, as well as those who make it a regular habit.

It is important for parents to understand and not burden young people with feelings of guilt, self-hatred and degradation. Especially must we avoid giving children and teens the impression that the sensations produced by the specialized nerve endings God has put within our bodies for pleasure are "bad"! At the same time, guidance in the use and control of sex should be emphasized.

Menopause

Sometimes called the "change of life," menopause is that time in life when a woman stops menstruating. It usually occurs between the age of forty-five and fifty, and takes place over several years. For two or three years during the forties or fifties a woman will notice increasing irregularity in her menstrual cycle before her periods cease entirely. This takes place because of a gradual decrease in the hormones produced in the ovaries, just as puberty began with an increase in these hormones. At the completion of the menopause, a woman's body no longer releases egg cells and she is no longer able to conceive and give birth to a child. Ovulation comes to a complete halt, and with it ends the menstrual cycle and monthly flow.

During the transition period, some women are fooled by the long intervals between menstrual periods and sometimes erroneously conclude that ovulation has ceased entirely before this is really true. Contraceptives are then given up, with the result that a surprise pregnancy may occur and a middle-aged couple unexpectedly is faced with the prospect of parenthood all over again. Children born in such situations are sometimes called "change-of-life babies." Doctors recommend that women allow at least two years to go by without a menstrual period before concluding that ovulation has ceased entirely.[47]

Many women pass through the menopause without unusual symptoms and difficulties—despite all the fears and myths that surround it. Sometimes there are mild physical symptoms, such as "hot flashes," fatigue or headaches. There may be psychological manifestations such as depression, irritability and crying spells. Much of this is due to the changes in the hormone pattern that takes place in bringing about the cessation of ovulation and menstruation. Where this is true, medical science can provide help through hormone treatment. Increasingly, physicians are realizing the value of estrogen therapy for many women, enabling them to pass through menopause without physical and emotional discomfort and distress.

On the other hand, a woman's mental attitude has a great deal to do with how she experiences menopause. If she worries about it beforehand, fearing it will make her "an old lady," or that it signals the end of all that matters in life, or that it will be a dreadful experience with all kinds of discomfort and physical suffering, then chances are that she'll have much more trouble than a woman who approaches it positively as a natural, normal event.

Women who have "lived" through their children, and who feel that childbearing is the purpose for which women were created and around which their lives should be centered, may have a particularly difficult time psychologically. They feel useless now that the childbearing years are over, and may have trouble developing new interests and self-esteem based upon other abilities beyond that of motherhood. Such women need patient understanding from their husbands and others to help them weather this period which seems so difficult. Another fear some women have is that menopause will decrease sexual desire and enjoyment. But this isn't true. In fact, many couples find sex after menopause, when the fear of pregnancy has disappeared, better than during earlier years.

Only in recent years has much attention been given to the question of whether or not men too undergo a "change of life." Although it is not as well understood as the female menopause, there is evidence that a male climacteric does exist. Men in their late fifties often experience hormonal withdrawal symptoms that may be compared to the hormone changes women undergo at menopause. Headaches, nervousness, fatigue and other symptoms are not uncommon and hormone therapy and other medications may be prescribed just as is the case with women. Many men become fearful of losing their sexual powers, and fail to understand that their *anxiety* can cause problems of impotence. If there is a healthy mental attitude toward this period of life, men can and do experience a healthy normal sex life all the way into old age.[48]

This Subject and Your Children

Small children aren't likely to ask about this, except to ask, "What's wrong with Grandma?" or, "What's the matter with Aunt Mary?" Usually a simple answer of "She's not feeling well. We must be extra loving and patient with her" will be enough to satisfy a small child.

Older children who understand the process of conception and birth to some extent may raise questions such as: "Does Grandma still produce eggs in her body that could grow into babies?" "How old is a woman when she can't have babies any longer?" "What is the change of life that people talk about? What is it that changes?" The facts about menopause mentioned above can be explained simply in ways children can understand.

Teen-agers' questions about menopause are usually concerned with a definition of the term and an understanding of what kinds of symptoms may occur. They may ask how problems of menopause are treated and how long menopause symptoms last. Some young people wonder if it's true that a woman's sex life ends at menopause, or if it's true that a woman's mental capacities are impaired at this stage. The answer to both questions is, "No, it's *not* true." Some teen-age girls may ask if, because they began menstruating early, say, at age eleven, it means they'll have an early menopause. Surprisingly, it's just the opposite. Usually, the menopause occurs earlier in women who began menstruating *later* rather than during the early teens or before.

Menstruation

Menstruation, from the Latin word *menstruus,* meaning "monthly," is the periodic discharge of a bloody fluid from the uterus through the vagina. Most girls and women speak of it as their "period." The *menarche,* or first menstruation, is the important biological event for a girl. It means that a hormone-controlled cycle has begun in her body which will continue until menopause is reached thirty or forty years later. Approximately every twenty-eight days she can expect her menstrual period to begin and to continue flowing for about three to five days. These are only the *averages,* and variation is to be expected. Some women have three-week cycles, others have five-week ones. Some girls and women have short periods lasting only two or three days, whereas others may menstruate for a full week. Such variations among women are perfectly normal. Also normal are the irregularities that occur in an individual woman from time to time. Some months a period may be a few days early, other months it may be a few days late. Emotional excitement, a cold, worry or shock, and other factors may throw a cycle off schedule and should not be a cause for worry. Irregularities and even missed periods are not unusual among young girls in the first year or so of menstruation. Even in older women a missed period is not *always* a sure indication of pregnancy, although this is the most common reason. Sometimes a period is delayed or even skipped for reasons connected with anemia or thyroid functioning.

To understand what is happening during menstruation, review chapters 5 and 7. You'll recall that approximately once a month an ovum or egg is released from one of the two ovaries and enters one of the Fallopian tubes. If it meets a sperm cell there and is fertilized, it moves into the uterus to become imbedded in a specially prepared soft lining of well-nourished tissue. There the fertilized ovum will grow for the next nine months until it is time to enter the world as a newborn baby.

On the other hand, if the ovum is *not* fertilized, it will disintegrate. In that case, the special inner lining in the

197

uterus won't be needed. The potential baby for whom it was intended as a nesting place never arrived. The "guest room" will have to be "redecorated" for the one who may possibly arrive the next month. Then the special lining, called the endometrium, begins to tear away from the underlying tissues which attach it to the walls of the uterus. Interlacing the special lining were many small blood vessels (capillaries). These are broken as the lining is being torn away and shed. The blood, along with mucus, tissue and a thin watery fluid that formed part of the nourishing lining, passes from the body in the form of menstrual fluid. Only about two ounces of blood are lost during the average menstrual period.

The process goes on over and over again during a woman's childbearing years. As soon as an old lining tears away, another new lining begins to grow in the uterus. The body keeps preparing for that baby that just might happen to begin. And if pregnancy does take place, the menstrual cycle (because of the amazing functioning of hormones) comes to a halt, to be resumed again usually about five to eight weeks after childbirth.

Christian parents may be disturbed to find that many educational materials on menstruation claim that the Bible presents an unhealthy and negative view of this bodily process. Primitive groups of past and present have blamed the presence of a menstruating woman for spoiled food, sour milk, blighting of crops, rusting of iron, bringing of diseases, and the presence of evil spirits; and it is also claimed that the Scriptures indicate a superstitious, fearful, unscientific view of menstrual periods. If one reads certain Bible passages, it's not hard to see where people get this idea. (See, for example, Leviticus 15:19-33; 20:18; Ezekiel 18:6; Isaiah 30:22, *KJV;* Ezekial 36:17,18; Lamentations 1:17, *KJV*.)

Under the ceremonial law of long-ago Israel, it is true that a woman was considered ritually "unclean" during

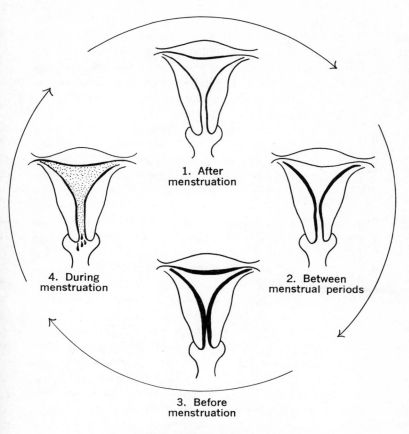

1. After menstruation

2. Between menstrual periods

3. Before menstruation

4. During menstruation

The uterus shown at various stages,
as the inner lining (endometrium) thickens and is shed.

Figure 18   The Menstrual Cycle

her menstrual period. She was expected to remain virtually isolated for seven days (cf. Leviticus 15:19 ff.) and was considered to spread contamination to anything or any person with whom she came into physical contact. If she lay on a bed, it became "unclean." If she sat on a chair, and someone else touched that chair, that person would also be considered "unclean" for the remainder of the day and would have to undergo special washings. The woman's husband was forbidden to have sexual intercourse with her during her period; otherwise, he too entered a state of "impurity" for seven days.

Such rules may seem puzzling and disturbing to us until we understand several things. First, ancient Hebrew law did not imply that there was literal "uncleanness", as did the views of the ancient Greeks and others, who thought a woman's body was ridding itself of poisons. The Hebrew idea of uncleanness was altogether different and was part of ceremonial law—*not* moral law. Ceremonial law included rules and rituals somewhat intermingled with health and sanitation measures, but mostly concerned with *holiness*. But the holiness and set-apartness God was teaching His people not only included moral and ethnical holiness; it also seems to have included some object lessons to get across the idea of holiness as *wholeness* and perfection or completion. British anthropologist Mary Douglas feels that this idea, along with the idea of holiness as also including *right order* (nothing out of place), provides the key for understanding some of the laws and rituals of ancient Israel.[49]

If this explanation is correct, the rules and ceremonies surrounding menstruation may have provided a picture of "not being physically whole," since the blood was departing from the woman's body, and of something "out of place" (again the blood)—which would furnish an illustration of "unholiness" as being *not whole* or complete. It did *not* mean that the woman herself as a person was unholy, impure and unclean. (Incidentally, lest it seem that women are being singled out, it should be noted that there were similar ceremonial rules regarding men who had an emission of semen. See the first part of Leviticus 15.)

Another possible explanation with regard to menstruation rules may relate to the awe with which the ancient Israelites regarded blood. Nations with fertility cults included rituals of drinking blood, but Israel was commanded to keep separate from blood. God wanted His people to view blood as something very special, the source of life and that which is given for atonement. (See Leviticus 17:11-14.) There was a sense of wonder, mystery, and almost fear in the way the Israelites regarded blood. This may be another way to explain some of the ceremonies connected with women and their periods.

However, we must remember that ceremonial washings, rituals and rules were done away with through our Lord Jesus Christ and what He did on the cross and at the tomb (cf. Hebrews 9:6—10:25). Christians today need not be troubled by such passages as those cited from Leviticus which were intended for a certain purpose among a certain people at a certain time.

It is interesting and comforting to realize that, at a time when many men feared contact with women because they just might happen to be menstruating, Jesus touched and commended the faith of a woman who had been in a state of ceremonial uncleanness for twelve years because of a menstrual disorder. (See Luke 8:43-48.)

This Subject and Your Children

Small children aren't apt to ask about menstruation, unless something comes up that opens up a discussion on the subject. That's what happened to one young mother when her three-year-old daughter and five-year-old son were helping her sort the wash. The little girl noticed some blood-stained panties lying among her mother's clothing and asked if "Mommy was hurt." Wisely and simply, the mother explained the menstruation process to her son and daughter. She helped them understand that the bleeding was *not* from a wound. But rather was the natural way a woman's body gets rid of the special material that the baby would have "nested in" if there had been a baby growing inside her. Reassured that Mommy wasn't hurt, the children accepted her explanation and went on helping her with the laundry.

Parents should make sure their daughter knows about menstruation before it happens, and some girls menstruate as early as ages nine or ten. In cases where girls were not told about menstruation in advance, its appearance has been terribly frightening and upsetting.

Sex educators recommend a positive approach when first discussing menstruation, tying the subject to the phenomenon of human growth and the wonder of becoming a woman. Children often talk about how tall they're becoming and other changes in their bodies. Such conversations can provide a starting point for discussing menstruation in a way that is natural and not awkward or strained. Young girls can learn that menstruation is one of the most important things that will happen as they grow toward womanhood. "God has specially designed women's bodies so they can someday be mothers," parents can say. "Even though it will be a long time until she will be married and have a baby, a girl's body begins preparing for the time when that will happen. Every month, a special lining grows inside her uterus or womb. That lining is soft, spongy and velvety, and is made to provide a nesting place and nourishment if a baby were to grow there. But when there isn't any baby there, the lining breaks apart because it isn't needed. It then flows out of the body through the special passageway between a woman's legs called the vagina. This is called menstruation or 'a period.' It's nothing to be afraid of—it's a natural, normal part of being a woman. Even though blood flows out, it doesn't mean you're injured or sick. Rather it's an indication of good health, that everything is functioning the way God planned when He designed women's bodies."

Don't, however, go overboard in glamorizing the process. Most girls and women don't go into ecstasies at the thought of their periods no matter how well they understand the process or marvel at the wonder of it all! Be honest in admitting that menstruating can seem to be a bother, but most women learn to take it in stride and think little of it. Show your daughter a sanitary belt and sanitary napkins (tampons, too, if desired) and explain how these are used.

Since the idea of menstruation seems a bit strange at first to most girls, they often wonder if girls have been cheated a bit to be made this way. A favorite question is, "Do boys have anything like menstruation?" Boys don't, of course, have anything quite like monthly periods because they don't ovulate, have a uterus or menstrual cycle. But their bodies do change. As manhood approaches, their sex organs are also being prepared for parenthood. You might want to tell your daughter about seminal emissions (review chapter 6) and explain that this is a new and somewhat strange experience for a boy the first time it happens, just as is a girl's first menstruation. It goes without saying that *sons* should know about nocturnal emissions well in advance of their occurrence, just as girls must be prepared for menstruation.

Boys should learn about menstruation around the same age girls learn about it. One mother found a ready-made opportunity as she and her son were driving home from grocery shopping. The boy noticed a box of sanitary napkins in one bag and commented, "Boy! The advertising gimmicks they think of to make you buy things! Those probably aren't any better or cleaner than any other kind of napkins, but they call them 'sanitary' so that people will pay more for them!" The mother realized the boy thought these were ordinary paper table napkins and then explained the real purpose of sanitary napkins.

Sometimes children who have pets will notice that bleeding takes place when their female cat or dog is in heat. They may ask if the animal is menstruating. The answer is no. The bleeding in this case indicates that ovulation has taken place and the animal can become pregnant. The period of heat or estrus, called rut in some animals, is the time when the female is most sexually receptive. With the exception of monkeys and apes, animals don't menstruate. The linings of most animals' uteruses are simply reabsorbed if pregnancy doesn't occur, rather than breaking down and passing from the body in the form of menstrual flow.[50]

Teen-age girls often have questions about whether or not they may wash their hair, take baths and showers, and exercise during their menstrual periods. The answer is yes to all of these questions. Cleanliness is especially important at this time, and in many instances exercise can be helpful in preventing or relieving cramps.

The exact cause of cramps isn't known. Some doctors believe physiological factors such as contractions of the uterus during the breakdown of the lining may be involved. Others believe that psychological factors play a part, especially among women who resent being a woman and have difficulty accepting the fact of menstruation. If cramps are a real problem to your daughter, ask your physician about it. He may prescribe medication or suggest a program of special exercises.

Other problems that sometimes occur in connection with menstruation are breast tenderness a few days before a period begins (this is normal and nothing to worry about), and a feeling of "blues" or depression as a period approaches. This occurs because hormones that have stimulated the thickening of the uterine lining also brought with them a general feeling of well-being. This feeling "goes away" as the hormones recede, leaving a woman feeling a bit letdown because of the contrast. Water retention is common at this time, too, because the body is retaining more salt. Often a girl feels heavy and bloated shortly before her period and this adds to the premenstrual tension. Weight gain at this time isn't apt to be an increase of fat but rather of extra fluid in the body. It will disappear when the period arrives.

Some teen-age girls may want to begin using tampons (internal menstrual protection)—especially for swimming, cheerleading, and the like. In most cases, the opening in the hymen through which the menstrual fluid passes will be large enough so that a tampon can be inserted without too much difficulty and without rupturing the hymen. Mothers should become familiar with the different types of tampons available, and should carefully read the detailed and well-illustrated directions that are provided in the tampon package before instructing daughters in their use.

Explaining menstruation to your children will be much easier if you take advantage of the excellent educational materials produced by the manufacturers of sanitary napkins and tampons. Helpful booklets are available at small cost or even free of charge. You might want to order the following:

From The Life Cycle Center
      Kimberly-Clark Corporation
      Neenah, Wisconsin 54956
Vol. I. "The Miracle of You"
Vol. II. "Your Years of Self-Discovery"

Vol. III. "You and Your Daughter"
Booklet: "Very Personally Yours"
(Price: 10¢ each)

From Director of Consumer Education
       Personal Products Company
       Box 6
       Milltown, New Jersey 08850
"Growing Up and Liking It" (for ages 9-14)
"Strictly Feminine" (for ages 14-22)
"How Shall I Tell My Daughter?"
(All copies free of charge.)

From Educational Department
       TAMPAX, Inc.
       5 Dakota Drive
       Lake Success, New York 11040
"Accent on You" (for girls up to 14 yrs.)
"It's Time You Knew" (for girls over 15)
(All copies free of charge)

Multiple Births

Children are frequently fascinated by the fact that a mother may give birth to twins, triplets, or even to quadruplets, quintuplets or sextuplets. The explanation is simple, and children of all ages will understand it if they already understand the basic facts of reproduction.

There are two ways that multiple births may occur. In some cases, a single ovum fertilized by a single sperm cell splits in half, or even into three or four parts. The resulting babies, since they came from the same fertilized ovum, will be of the same sex, have the same heredity and will look very much alike. Such multiple births are called *identical.*

In other cases, more than one egg is released from the ovaries during a single menstrual cycle. One ovary may produce more than one egg at a time, or *both* ovaries may produce eggs. Different sperm cells may then fertilize each of the eggs, and the resultant multiple birth will be called *fraternal*. Fraternal twins or triplets look no more alike than do any other brothers and sisters. They just happen to have been born during the same birth rather than at separate times.

Multiple births may occur in either of these ways or there might be a combination of them. One family might have a set of identical twins (both babies from one fertilized egg cell)—two look-alike boys or girls. Another family might have a set of triplets in which none of the babies look alike. There might be, for example, three boys from three different egg cells, or a boy and two girls all from different egg cells. A third family might have a set of triplets in which two of the children are identical (two girls from a single cell), and a third child which is fraternal, who could be either a boy or girl. Or a set of quadruplets might contain two sets of identical "twins."

There are a few cases of twins in the Bible, the most famous of which are Jacob and Esau, the sons of Isaac and Rebekah (see Genesis 25:21-26). Genesis 38:27-30 describes the birth of another set of twins. In the New Testament, evidently the apostle Thomas was a twin. He was often called "Didymus" which means "the twin" (John 11:16; 20:24).

Nudity

The Bible emphasizes the sanctity of the human body as a marvelous example of God's handiwork. Never is the body presented as an object of shame, scorn, or ridicule. And it is never to be treated with disdain or embarrassment. We know God designed our bodies, and the human form is very beautiful. This is something artists have long recognized as they have sought to capture the unclothed beauty of the human body in paintings and sculpture.

Why then do humans wear clothing? Why cover up our bodies if they are so wonderful? The most obvious reason is the practical one. The need for warmth, comfort, protection. Clothing has a functional purpose. Even nudist camps recognize this when they permit sunglasses, sandals, and hats to provide shade during sunbathing. The practical side of clothing, of course, varies according to climate; but it is an important factor in explaining why nudity isn't more widely practiced.

There are social reasons for clothing, too, completely apart from the sexual aspect. Clothing is a way of presenting ourselves to others, packaged in a certain kind of image we want to project. Clothing can reflect social status or have special meaning (like a military uniform). It may be a way of calling attention to our own unique tastes and personality. Pride, selfishness, and a love of materialism can easily enter here; and Christians should be aware that there can be just as much sin involved in the wearing of clothing as in their removal.

The main reason people in our society wear clothing has to do with sex. Uncovering the body means exposing the sex organs, which in turn arouses people to sensuality and lust. This explains the preference for clothing far more than even the functional explanation. After all, it would be possible to keep warm in special see-through fabrics or clear plastic! In our particular culture it is a rare sight to see a mother nursing her baby because the female breast has become such a sex object that a woman hesitates to expose it publicly even when it's fulfilling its most basic purpose.

Not all cultures see things this way. Nudity doesn't have strong sexual meaning everywhere. As M. O. Vincent has expressed it, "In nude cultures, nudity is not lewdity."[51] Not wearing clothing in such societies does not mean there will be sexual promiscuity. Often strict sex codes are observed. Elisabeth Elliot refers to this in a description of her work as a missionary among the Auca Indians of Ecuador:

"In my country we hold certain standards of dress to be acceptable for a few months or a year at a time. But a costume that would have landed its wearer in jail one year might be common on the streets of a city the next. The Aucas were unhampered by clothing (or by washing, sewing, mending, or ironing) and the caprices of fashion (with the vanity, jealousy, covetousness and discontent which fashion fosters), but stuck firmly to a code of modesty which did not change with the seasons. In their nakedness they accepted themselves and one another for what they were, always abiding by the rules: men and women did not bathe together, women taught their daughters how to sit and stand with modesty, men taught their sons how to wear the string which was their only adornment. Physiological functions were discussed in public but performed in strictest privacy."[52]

The question then arises: What does the Bible have to say about nudity? The earliest reference is to Adam and Eve in the garden. "The man and his wife were both naked, and were not ashamed" (Genesis 2:25). Yet, things changed after they disobeyed God's commandment. They became ashamed of their nakedness and tried to hide from the eyes of God, covering themselves with fig leaves. Why? This was not so much physical shame. They had been unclothed in the presence of God and each other before. But rather a sense of *spiritual* exposure—a sense of being guilty before God, with a sense of something missing, something having been stripped away. They could no longer feel at ease before His eyes. They hoped that covering their physical bodies might be a way of hiding, of covering their sin. But that never works. "Not a creature exists that is concealed from His sight, but all things are open and exposed, naked and defenseless to the eyes of Him with Whom we have to do," (Hebrews 4:13, *Amplified*). God, however, understood how they felt, and provided them with animal skins as coverings, perhaps as an indication that there can be no atonement and reconciliation with God apart from the shedding of blood. (See Hebrews 9:22.)

The "shame of nakedness" in the sense of being spiritually stripped and exposed is also what is meant in Revelation 3:18.

There are other passages in Scripture with explicit regard to physical nakedness. The Levitical laws forbid the "uncovering of the nakedness" of anyone other than one's own spouse (cf. Leviticus 18:6 ff.). The incident in Genesis 9:20 ff., where drunken Noah committed a breach of modesty and uncovered himself (the Hebrew suggests it was a deliberate act), may have sexual connotations. His son saw and talked about it to his brothers and there is a hint of impurity in the thought life if not in actual conduct.

Yet the Bible presents no sense of shame in describing the delight of husband and wife as they enjoy one another's naked bodies in the marital embrace. Passages in the Song of Solomon and the fifth chapter of Proverbs make this clear. It is not nudity in itself that is wrong, but rather its meaning in a particular culture and the context in which it occurs. Nude tribes may, for example, consider it wrong for a woman to remove her tiny grass skirt in the presence of another woman while giving birth to a child, or may consider it "indecent exposure" for a man to take off his tiny G-string, except in the presence of his wife. Some tribes have been dismayed when missionaries insisted women's breasts be covered, because in these cultures the bare breast signified purity whereas the covered breast indicated prostitution!

This Subject and Your Children

Most sex educators feel a casual, relaxed attitude toward the body is important. Privacy and modesty can be taught because we live in a society where public nudity is for the most part unacceptable. On the other hand we shouldn't convey to youngsters a sense of shame or embarrassment about their bodies. In some homes, both parents and children feel entirely comfortable about seeing one another nude. In other homes, privacy and modesty might be stressed more.

The topic of how much of the body should be exposed comes up with teen-agers in connection with current fads. Parents should keep in mind how attitudes change on the subject. It wasn't too long ago that some Christians believed sleeveless dresses were sinful. At the same time we can emphasize that a degree of modesty is never out of style. If we know that certain body gestures or ways of dressing are provocative and can cause others to think wrong thoughts, we must be careful for their sake, if not for our own. However, even this "weaker brother" argument (cf. Romans 14:13-21) has limits. In one extreme example, the dean of a Christian school, not too many years ago, insisted girls wear stockings because "bare legs would cause boys to think sinful thoughts." Later she called a meeting to tell the girls they must wear stockings with *seams* because one male student told her he found himself staring at the legs of coeds with seamless hose wondering if their legs were covered!

The question of nude mixed swimming sometimes comes up among modern young people. The practice is often said to be part of the younger generation's search for honesty in human relationships or a desire to unmask psychologically, so that the real person is seen for what he or she truly is, free from hypocrisy, pretense or role-playing. It's argued that in the state of nakedness, people see one another exactly as they are; and also there's the added point that all humans look very much alike when one gets down to the "bare facts."

The search for honesty and openness is to be commended, but reaching such a point in human relationships takes more than stripping off one's clothes. Young people should be helped to see that it's far better to save the unveiling of one's physical self until the wedding night when the bodies of husband and wife can be enjoyed together in the way God intended.

Petting

Petting is usually defined as sexually stimulating physical contact between persons of the opposite sex. Sometimes the term is used in a broad general sense, covering all aspects of physical contact from a hug and light goodnight kiss all the way through to mutual masturbation. Just as long as the physical contact does not include actual sexual intercourse, i.e., the penetration of the vagina by the penis. But usually the term *petting* is reserved for only the more intimate forms of premarital sex play. Thus, adolescents distinguish between "necking" and "petting" behavior. Necking has been said to refer to that which goes on "above the neck," and petting "that which goes on below the neck." Of course, it isn't hard to find some errors in that distinction. After all, holding hands isn't thought of as particularly erotic behavior, yet it takes place "below the neck." And deep, tongue-kissing (the "French kiss") can be extremely sexually arousing, yet it takes place "above the neck." So the matter isn't as simple as it appears at first glance.

On the other hand, some distinctions have to be made —whether one sees the whole process as a continuum of progression or as two separate types of behavior. The continuum idea makes more sense and seems more accurate. No one can deny the vast difference in premarital behavior between the boy and girl who at the end of a date embrace briefly and kiss one another good night, as opposed to a couple who fondle each other's genitals in petting sessions in the back seat of a car.

Some social scientists view the increase in petting practices as one of the most noteworthy changes in sexual behavior patterns among young people. Petting to orgasm seems to have come upon the scene suddenly and the practice has rapidly spread. In this sense, it has been called "revolutionary" by some, in contrast to the incidence of actual intercourse, where the rise has been more gradual and "evolutionary" (part of a continuing trend which began in the 1920's) rather than something sudden. Others, however, are quick to point out that petting isn't something new either. Past generations practiced it in one form or another under such names as "sparking," "spooning" and "bundling," although such practices may not have included petting to climax.

When parents were growing up, their parents and church leaders warned them about petting dangers. The most serious being that petting could cause a couple to become so sexually stimulated they might "lose control and go all the way." The new generation views the matter differently. They feel they've discovered how to "go all the way" *without* "going *all* the way." That is, they practice some form of mutual masturbation so that an orgasm is reached and sexual gratification is felt. At the same time they can pride themselves on having refrained from intercourse. Sexual experience is gained, but virginity is preserved. It seems like a good "have-your-cake-and-eat-it" solution, and a large number of youth, including young people from strong Christian homes, Christian colleges, and biblically sound churches, engage in such conduct. On the other hand, there are those who conclude that if they're going that far there would hardly be any difference in going all the way.

"Technical virginity" is the term sometimes used for

213

both women and men who engage in extremely intimate sex play, yet stop short of sexual union. The reasoning being that such a person's "virginal state" is merely a technicality. Petting behavior in such cases may include fondling and oral stimulation of a girl's breasts, touching and rubbing one another's genitals, the placing of bare genitals together but avoiding penetration, and oral-genital contact (both fellatio and cunnilingus, defined under Homosexuality in this chapter; also both types simultaneously in the position young people refer to by the slang expression, "Sixty-nine").

Most parents will recognize that what youth has discovered in all this is simply marital foreplay. The only difference is that efforts are directed toward experiencing sexual climax apart from the complete act.

This Subject and Your Children

Young children usually regard the boy-girl hugging and kissing they see on TV or in public displays as amusing, mushy, gushy and something to giggle about. But as puberty approaches, the subject is understood in a different light.

If lines of communication between parents and children have been kept open, parents should discuss the pitfalls of petting. Opportunities may arise, as through a newspaper "doctor's column," in which it isn't unusual to read a question from a troubled teen who wonders if it's possible to become pregnant while still technically a virgin. Or if it's possible to contract a venereal disease through genital intimacy short of intercourse. The answer to both questions is yes. If a boy ejaculates at the opening of a girl's vagina, it is possible in rare cases for sperm cells to enter and swim upward, resulting in conception. And if one of the persons is infected with syphilis, it's even possible for the germ to be transmitted through French kissing.

214

Although teen-agers should be aware of such facts, there is certainly much more to be considered in the light of Christian moral standards. What the whole petting question boils down to is this: How much sex is permissible before marriage? In trying to work out an answer with teens, you might want to keep the following considerations in mind:

1. 1 Corinthians 6:9-20 and 1 Thessalonians 4:1-8 make it clear that the believer's sex life is important to God. Romans 12:1,2 reminds us that as Christians we need not (should not, must not) conform to the world's standards. At the same time, we must recognize the Scriptures provide no specific rules on line-drawing, degrees of intimacy, or other human regulations. There are no commandments such as, "Thou shalt not hold hands until the third date." Instead we must look for principles and guidelines.

2. The familiar question, "How far can I go?" must be viewed in the context of the particular relationship. If *casual dating* is in view and the couple is just getting to know each other, why should necking and petting be looked upon as an expectation if not a requirement? Must a girl feel she should in some way "pay" for the date with her body? If a boy and girl scarcely know each other as persons, do they have the right to try to "know" one another's bodies? If seeking pleasure and experience is the goal, isn't that using or exploiting the other person for selfish ends? On the other hand, if a couple is seriously committed to one another in a relationship that in all probability is leading toward marriage, they will undoubtedly desire to physically express their affection to one another. In this situation, it is a physical expression of *affection* which makes it different from a parking session in casual dating with whomever one happens to be out with on a particular evening. But even in a serious relationship such as engagement, it's not a matter of

"anything goes." The question of "How far?" must still be faced.

3. If the scriptural warnings against fornication are taken seriously, and if fornication refers to sexual relations between unmarried persons, then we must ask ourselves if there's a relationship between fornication and petting. Shouldn't petting be viewed as part of the act of intercourse? In marriage, foreplay isn't just "the preliminaries" before the "real thing." Rather, it's all part of the one-flesh relationship in its physical expression.

4. 1 Corinthians 7:4 makes clear that sexual access to a person's body is only the right of one's spouse. Reciprocal rights to a body of the opposite sex belong only to those who have entered the one-flesh marriage commitment. If this is so, then it would follow that those areas of the body which are especially designed for erotic arousal and stimulation should not be shared with another person before marriage. All the biblical imagery about reserving one's "fountain" or not sharing "one's nakedness" with another outside marriage seems to make clear that this is the ideal. There is something very special and beautiful about "unveiling" oneself to one's beloved on the wedding night after the bond has been publicly legalized. This line of reasoning rules out the permissibility of the intimate forms of premarital petting discussed earlier. Such petting should be seen as part of intercourse, not something separate.

5. The matter of strategy should be mentioned. It is wise for a couple to determine in advance how far they believe physical expressions of affection should go. And it's also wise to have plans about how to avoid sexually stimulating situations where it would be hard to stop. Some Christian couples are able to discuss these matters openly and to work out guidelines so each knows how far things will be permitted to go as the relationship progresses. They might determine that physical contact

will be limited in the early stages of the relationship in order to know one another as persons. Perhaps they will feel only light kissing is appropriate before engagement because they want their kisses to have a very special meaning later. After engagement, they might feel deeper kissing and embracing are in order, yet avoiding the uncovering or direct stimulation of more intimate parts. If they've determined such guidelines in advance, it may make it much easier than just letting whatever "happens" happen. There are, however, no rules on this. It's a matter of Christian liberty between the individual couple and God.

6. Parents should also be aware of the tremendous pressures put upon young people by peers encouraging them to engage in permissive sex behavior. There are some adults who write articles encouraging intimate petting, who say it's necessary for learning sex techniques. "Since," they say, "there won't be as much time or opportunity for that in marriage"! One would think a leisurely honeymoon and the long years of married life would furnish far more opportunities to learn and grow together sexually than would a hurried, guarded rendezvous in the back seat of a car.

Both boys and girls feel such pressures which are often a far greater problem than *physical* tensions. Young people need support and encouragement to help them to avoid succumbing to sexual temptation. Research among an often-neglected group, virginal boys, indicates they face tremendous pressures among peers who urge them to "demonstrate their masculinity and maturity" through sexual adventures. Pressures are especially great in the military and college. Older males with whom young men may work during summer jobs or after-school employment often make it rough for those without sexual experience, implying that "something's wrong with them" if they haven't yet tried intercourse.[53]

Girls, too, are pressured because of a society that has too long insisted women should be sex objects rather than developing as persons. One Christian boy in college said he wishes petting weren't such a common practice because he'd rather not do it, yet feels compelled to. "When I date Christian girls," he says, "they're disappointed if there's no petting—even on the earliest dates. I've even had *Christian* girls tell me that they want me to fondle their breasts the very first time I'm out with them!" A girl, on her part, often fears that if a boy doesn't make sexual advances it must mean she lacks "sex appeal." Christian parents and youth leaders can help young people see what's wrong with this kind of thinking. Help them sort things out so the whole matter of petting and premarital sex can be viewed in Christian perspective.

Pornography

The word "pornography" comes from the Greek word *porneia* which as we saw earlier is found many times in the New Testament and is usually translated "fornication" or "immorality." Literally, the Greek word *pornographos* means "writing about harlots." Reading materials, pictures, drawings, movies and photographs which portray the sex act in a depersonalized way, are classified as pornographic. These are always separated from human affection and the institution of marriage, and are designed to stir up fantasies and provide substitute gratification. There is some confusion, however, about the definition. And despite court cases, there is confusion about whether certain materials are "obscene" or "pornographic" or whether they have "socially redeeming value" despite explicit descriptions of sexual activities. Some judges use the term "hard-core pornography" to designate "material which can be legally suppressed."[54] In the general usage of the term, hard-core pornography

218

is considered to be "under-the-counter" materials. Broadly speaking, pornography would include "girlie" magazines, stag films and "skin flicks" shown in special "adults-only" movie theaters and books sold in "adult bookstores."

Pornographic pictures to which young people and adults may be exposed include pictures of nude adults engaged in sex play, heterosexual intercourse, homosexual relations, and sado-masochistic activities involving whippings, spankings, and other efforts to connect sex with physical pain and torture. Pornographic literature includes stories and vivid descriptions of wild sex parties, orgies, and acts of sadism and masochism (sexual gratification through physical pain and humiliation).

This Subject and Your Children

Children who receive a good sex education and who can openly discuss their questions about sex with their parents are far less likely to turn to pornographic materials than are children whose parents rely on fear and ignorance as the means of preventing sexual misconduct. When their natural curiosity about sex is not satisfied in an intelligent manner and reinforced by positive sexual values, children may look to pornography to answer their questions. The sad thing is they get wrong answers, misleading information, and an unwholesome view of sex that separates it from love and marriage.

Don't be surprised if your children come into contact with pornographic materials. One child from a Christian home ran into his house to show his parents a tiny viewer a playmate brought to show his friends. Fortunately, the three- and four-year-olds were more fascinated with the gadget than with the inside picture of a nude woman in a provocative pose. The Christian parents explained to their son that God had created the human body to be very beautiful and special. But that sometimes people made fun of the body and treated it wrongly. And some men treated women in very wrong ways. Pictures like the one in the viewer are not pleasing to God because they can make us think about His good gifts in wrong ways.

Discussing the subject and building into children positive attitudes toward sex is far better than trying to "protect" them so that they'll never find out about such materials. One ten-year-old boy from a Christian home, where sex education had been provided since his earliest days, told of visiting a schoolmate's home. His friend had taken him to a special locked closet. "My dad thinks I don't know this stuff is here," he said, "but I found where he hides the key and when my parents aren't home I come in here and look at the pictures." He opened the door and pulled out a stack of *Playboy* magazines. The boys looked at them. The one who had access to informative sex education materials at home, who had open communication in his family, and whose parents tried to provide him with scriptural guidelines soon lost interest. When he arrived home he told his parents about it. They didn't act shocked nor scold him for looking at the magazines, but discussed the matter briefly, then dropped the subject.

It's a good idea to help your youngsters see the difference between art and pornography. Help them understand that the nude body seen at the museum in a famous painting or in the form of a statue is quite different than the naked body shown in a sensuous pose in a girlie magazine. Intent and meaning make the difference.

In discussing the subject with teen-agers, point out how depersonalized sex is in pornography. How it doesn't depict a relationship of *persons,* but rather emphasizes genital contact totally apart from the context of affection, love and commitment between human beings. Sex just for the sake of sex becomes boring, and creators of pornography recognize this. That's why they try to inject a variety of strange exotic, often sick, technology to the sex act.

Teen-agers also should understand the effects pornography has on their thought life and should avoid it if they want to sincerely pray: "Let the words of my mouth and the meditation of my heart be acceptable in thy sight, O Lord, my rock and my redeemer" (Psalm 19:14). According to one definition, pornography is material "to be read or seen with one hand,"[55] that is, as an accompaniment to masturbation. For a Christian young person to use such materials to stimulate autoerotic fantasies would be to go against all that the Bible says sex can and should be.

Prostitution

A prostitute is a person who, for a price, engages in sex relations with a variety of "clients" or "customers." Usually the term "prostitute" is associated with females who are sometimes called whores, harlots, call girls or streetwalkers. But there are also male prostitutes who usually engage in homosexual practices for pay. Female prostitutes for the most part have sex relations with men although a small percentage may engage in lesbian activities.

A house or apartment where prostitutes carry on their business is known as a brothel, and the woman in charge of it is known as a madam. The man who solicits customers and shares the prostitutes' earnings is known as a pimp. Prostitutes refer to their customers as "johns" or "tricks." Not all professional prostitutes work in brothels; some are streetwalkers, soliciting their customers in bars and on streets. Then there are more sophisticated prostitutes who like to think of themselves as being in another class from the others. These are the "call girls" who obtain their clients through individual referral and who make most of their contacts over the telephone. Call girls are usually quite attractive and worldly-wise, expensive, and entertain their customers in their own apartments or the hotel room where a man is staying during a business trip.

Prostitution has existed all through history. One of the earliest Bible stories related to the subject is found in Genesis 38:13-26. Warnings against prostitution in the Levitical laws referred to the temple prostitution associated with idolatry and the fertility cults (cf. Deuteronomy 23:17,18). In the book of Proverbs there are many warnings to young men about the dangers of prostitutes and adulteresses. The book of Hosea describes how the prophet married a prostitute, at the command of God, to illustrate God's continued love for Israel despite her unfaithfulness. In the New Testament, Jesus ignored the self-righteous complaints of the Pharisee and showed compassion on a prostitute, extending to her His forgiveness, cleansing and healing (cf. Luke 7:36-50). However, contrary to popular thought, there is no biblical evidence that Mary Magdalene was ever a prostitute.

This Subject and Your Children

If children ask what a prostitute is, you can explain according to the above, taking care to point out that this is a wrong use of God's gift of sex and of the body. It's very sad that some women do this. Often it's because of a poor childhood, lack of education, training and guidance. Sometimes young girls get into prostitution because they're addicted to drugs and feel it's the only way they can earn money to buy more. Other young women are attracted to the vocation because it seems to promise high pay, nice clothes and expensive gifts.

Teen-age boys sometimes may hear their friends talk about visiting houses of prostitution, but often such stories are made up to impress their peers. Studies indicate that decreasing numbers of young boys and young men visit prostitutes for their first sexual experience. More often the clientele consists of over-thirty and middle-aged men, a large number of whom are married, but for one reason or another have failed to find sexual satisfaction with their wives.

Rape

The word rape comes from a Latin term meaning to "seize or snatch." It is an act of physical violence in which a woman is forced to have sexual intercourse against her will. The term "statutory rape" is used in cases where a man has sex relations with a girl (even if she agreed to the act), if the girl is below the legal age of consent (which varies from state to state). If a woman persuades a boy or man to have sexual intercourse with her, she is *seducing* him, not raping him. A man can force sexual intercourse upon a woman because of the way her body is made. But a woman cannot *force* a man into sexual relations with her; he must first have an erection before intercourse is possible for him.

Two of the best-known examples of rape in the Bible are the story of the rape of Jacob's daughter, Dinah (Genesis 34) and the rape of Tamar, daughter of David, by her own brother (2 Samuel 13). A horrible crime of violent mob rape is described in Judges 19:22-30. Young Joseph was falsely accused of rape in Genesis 39:6-20. Among the ancient Israelites, the crime of raping a betrothed girl was punishable by death (Deuteronomy 22:25-27). If, however, a girl was not betrothed, the man who forced her was required to marry her (Deuteronomy 22:28,29).

This Subject and Your Children

Children who happen to hear the term "rape" may be told simply that it means a man has been cruel to a woman and hurt her body. Older children who have a better understanding of sexual intercourse can be given a more specific definition.

Understandably, adults are very concerned about and fearful of sex crimes against children. Yet care must be taken not to arouse unnecessary fright and suspicion in youngsters by vague warnings about "strangers." Actually, many sexual encounters between adults and children involve acquaintances. Sex educators suggest that children be helped to understand the appropriate kinds of circumstances in which strangers can be met, rather than condemning all strangers.

Through proper sex education, children can be helped to understand their bodies and can come to understand that certain acts, gestures, and desires to touch them on the part of others, is wrong. Parents should not panic if a child tells of such things, but should comfort and reassure him. Many victims of sexual acts report that the reactions of adults frightened and harmed them in almost a greater way than the original act. Unfortunately, even some police departments and courts add to the emotional trauma of a child after sex crimes have been reported.

Several years ago, an eight-year-old girl was abducted by a child molester who kept her overnight, then returned her to her home the next morning unharmed. Her parents and various authorities were persuaded that the child's upbringing which included a positive attitude toward sex and toward other people, and emphasis on being calm and unafraid, may have saved her life. The child understood what was going on throughout the ordeal, yet remained clearheaded, poised and composed. Because she didn't panic, neither did her kidnapper. After sobering up (he had been drinking heavily), he became rational enough to take the child home.[56]

A medical journal advises physicians called in on cases

of rape to give more attention to the psychological and emotional needs of the victim and her parents. Girls who have been raped should be helped by calm reassurance. What has happened should not be blown up in such a way that the girl and her parents are made to feel that something irreversible has occurred which can never be remedied, that the girl has "lost her virginity" and is somehow "spoiled" for marriage. Rather, "it is often a therapeutic maneuver to compare a sexual assault with an ordinary physical assault. Both are initially terrifying and at times painful, but with both the effect is not irreversible and time will heal."[57] And for the Christian, not only time but, much more than that, *God* provides healing and can remove the hurt of both heart and body.

Sex Slang

Everybody knows there are certain words that are considered vulgar and obscene. People speak of them as "gutter language," "filthy talk," "dirty words," or "four-letter words." These words are tremendously potent and so upsetting to people that many of them are not yet found in dictionaries and only recently have begun appearing in print or on the motion picture screen.

Why is it that a certain combination of letters of the alphabet can have such force for shock? Because words in any language are symbols of communication. Obscene words are words that communicate feelings about natural bodily processes and body parts. If you stop to analyze it, words considered "dirty" are words relating to the organs of sex and of excretion (the emptying of the bladder and intestines). There's an emotional reaction of shock and repugnance to having our attention called to these forbidden or repressed areas of life. In some persons, speaking or hearing them may arouse sexual excitement.

A theater critic has suggested that vulgar terms might

be thought of as "reverse euphemisms." A euphemism is a nice way of saying something unpleasant and thereby taking some of the ugliness or pain out of it. For example we say, "He passed away" instead of "He died," or "The child threw up," instead of "He vomited." A *reverse* euphemism would be taking something that is good and beautiful and describing it in a way that makes it seem coarse and ugly.

Bawdiness or lewd talk is likely to appear in any language. It's nothing new to our age. The early Christians ran up against crude jokes, risque remarks, and gutter talk scrawled on walls much like the graffiti found today. During the time of Nero, Petronius published his ribald comedy *The Satyricon* which shows that the people of Rome made use of "four-letter words." Christians were instructed to steer clear of such talk. They were constantly reminded that the body is holy and that sex is a wonderful creation and gift of God—not something to be toyed with or made fun of. Thus the Ephesians were instructed, "Dirty stories, foul talk, and coarse jokes—these are not for you. Instead, remind each other of God's goodness and be thankful" (Ephesians 5:4, *TLB*).

Since vulgar language is common, parents should understand what the terms mean so that they can answer questions their children might have upon hearing such words. Here are some of the most common ones:

Words relating to male physiology. The penis in street talk may be called a prick, cock, pecker, dick, rod, or meat. The testicles are referred to as nuts or balls. Erections are called "boners" or "hard-ons," and ejaculation is spoken of as "coming" or "shooting off." The semen is called "the come."

Words relating to female physiology. A girl's vulva in crude language may be referred to as a "pussy." Her vagina is spoken of as a "cunt" or "box." The clitoris is called "the clit," "tingler," "button" or "switch." The hymen is called a "cherry." Breasts are referred to as "tits," "boobs," or "boobies."

Words relating to petting and sexual intercourse. "Making out" is not usually considered a vulgar expression, but its meaning seems to vary in various places. To some young people the words merely mean necking and/ or petting; to others, the term might suggest sexual intercourse. On the other hand, the expression "making love" *does* refer to sexual intercourse, as does the expression "making it." "Making love" isn't considered a vulgar term. Boys who pet a great deal and have erections without orgasms sometimes complain of a pain in the groin and use such expressions as "lover's nuts" or "stone ache." If a man has intercourse with a virgin, he may refer to it as "picking a cherry." Slang and vulgar terms for having sexual intercourse in general may include "sleep with," "ball," "lay (or get laid)," "hump," "score," "screw," and "fuck." To have an orgasm is "to come."

Miscellaneous sex slang words. Masturbation (in boys) is called "jacking off," "jerking off," or "beating your meat." If a girl becomes pregnant she is said to be "knocked up." There are slang and street terms for venereal diseases, too. Someone with gonorrhea may be said to have "the clap," "the drip," "the strain," or "the whites." Passing on gonorrhea to someone else is to give that person "a dose." Common terms for the other major venereal disease, syphilis, are "syph," "the blues," or "bad blood."

This Subject and Your Children

Children may use obscenity as an attention-getting device. Or they may wish to test the reaction of adults or other children. Sometimes they use vulgar expressions as part of their curiosity about sex. And sometimes the words are used quite innocently; the child has heard a new term somewhere and without knowing or understanding its meaning adds it to his vocabulary.

Some parents react with amusement when a tiny child utters a four-letter word and comment on "how cute" it seems. Obviously such an approach will only encourage a child to use such language and gain the reputation of being a person with a "foul mouth." At the opposite extreme are those parents who are shocked and horrified to hear their child speak such a word. Often they indicate their displeasure by threatening or punishing the child. Frequently the child hasn't the slightest idea what the word means. The best way to handle the situation is to calmly explain what the word means and why we shouldn't use it. This, too, can be part of sex education in the home.

Sex Thoughts and Fantasies

Everybody thinks about sex at some time or another. Sex is an important part of our human nature, part of the way God created us. Yet, many people think that *any* thinking about sex is wrong—that the expressions "evil thoughts" or "impurity in the thought life" always refer to sex. They feel guilty and ashamed and desperately try to rid themselves of sex thoughts, hoping to repress them or run away from them. Yet sex thoughts don't seem to disappear. Jerome, one of the early church fathers, complained that even though he fled to a desert wilderness, wept and fasted, he "fancied (himself) amongst bevies of dancing maidens," with his mind "burning with the cravings of desire, and the fire of lust flared up from (his) flesh."[58]

Some sex educators and psychiatrists feel that there are positive benefits in all kinds of fantasy and daydreams, like savoring the joy of an imaginary journey, honor, romance, or act of heroism. Daydreams can be both a means of *pleasure* and a way of *planning* for the future—a way of mentally trying something out and thinking through how one would act before the experience takes place.[59] In this way, sex fantasies can be good.

On the other hand, what is the Christian to say about Christ's warning in Matthew 5:27,28, where He tells us that it's possible to commit sexual sin in the thought life? One can commit murder, pride, greed, envy and other kinds of sins in the mind, as well. (See Matthew 5:21,22; 1 John 3:15; Matthew 12:34-37; Mark 7:21-23.) Therefore, we must take Christ's warning about mental adultery seriously and make a conscious effort not to think *wrong* kinds of thoughts about sex.

Wrong thoughts are any thoughts in which we imagine ourselves participating in sexual conduct clearly forbidden in the Word of God. It is wrong for a Christian to fantasize that he is participating in an orgy, adultery, fornication, sadomasochistic acts, bestiality (sexual relations with an animal; see Leviticus 20:15,16), or homosexual activities. Or that he is engaging in sex relations with a particular person whom he has been "lusting after." All of these types of sex daydreams occur among human beings, and their occurrence shouldn't make anyone feel that he or she is somehow abnormal, degraded and apt to commit some vile sex crime. On the other hand, in view of scriptural teachings about the thought life, they should, for the Christian, be regarded as sinful.

Other problems and dangers that might occur in uncontrolled sex fantasies could include preoccupation with daydreaming to the detriment of other areas of life, such as not doing well in schoolwork, performing poorly on a job, or thinking about sex so much that sex tensions are increased and the likelihood of *acting* upon one's "dreams" becomes a real possibility.

This Subject and Your Children

Parents should be aware that thinking about sex is perfectly normal. This is particularly true of junior-high and high-school-age young people whose bodies are developing in such a way that all sorts of new and exciting urges and feelings are being experienced.

Don't expect teens to tell you their sex thoughts. (Remember when you were a teen-ager?) But you can put them at ease by helping them feel that there's nothing "impure" or "dirty" about wondering and imagining what sex relations are like. Show them that such thoughts are part of growing up. A boy might be shocked to find himself suddenly wondering what his English teacher looks like in the nude. A girl might be attending a wedding and suddenly find that her mind is racing ahead to the couple's honeymoon and marriage bed. Teen-agers may sometimes put themselves to sleep at night imagining what sex would be like. Such fantasies, incidentally, are not always accompanied by masturbation. There are some teens who never masturbate but make up sexual daydreams.

You can help teens to understand that the right kinds of sex thoughts aren't evil. This can avoid guilt feelings on the one hand and eliminate roundabout ways of seeking sex pleasure on the other. For example, sometimes young people imagine themselves being *forced* into sex relations and can thus pretend they're experiencing sex without its being any fault of their own. This is especially true of some girls who want to daydream about sex, yet are convinced it's wrong. Therefore they make up fantasies about being carried off and raped, or of being ravished by a group of soldiers in a raid or wartime prison. Obviously these aren't healthy ways to dream about sex.

Some practical helps with regard to sex and the thought life are these:

1. Recognize that wrong thoughts about sex may sometimes pop into our minds. We can't help that; it's

what we do with them that matters. Remember the old saying that "you can't stop birds from flying over your head, but you don't have to let them build a nest in your hair."

2. Keep busy in all sorts of worthwhile activities so that excessive daydreaming isn't permitted to become a problem.

3. Pray about it. Jesus understands our temptations and promises to help immediately as we call on Him in time of need (Hebrews 4:15,16). Ask His help *at the very moment* the wrong thought comes to mind. "Lord Jesus, please help me to keep my thoughts pleasing to You." "Lord, I'm not thinking about that girl (that boy) in the way I should. I'm having wrong desires. Give me Your strength so that I can resist the temptation to let these thoughts go any further." One young missionary wrote that when he was tempted to think lustful thoughts about a girl, he'd immediately start praying for her. He prayed that her spirit might be as beautiful as her body and that she might come to know Christ as Saviour and Lord, and that her body might become the temple of the Holy Spirit. He said that when he finished praying that way, all lustful thoughts toward the girl disappeared! Biblical examples of prayers for the thought life are found in Psalm 19:12-14 and 139:23,24.

4. Meditate on Scripture. (See Psalms 1:2; 119:9-11.)

5. Make a conscious effort to think good thoughts, and that can include good thoughts about sex. That means thinking of sex from *God's* point of view, keeping in mind biblical standards, and realizing God's design for sex within marriage. That means that we must keep close watch on our thoughts and bring them into line if they stray from what's pleasing to God. "We take every thought captive and make it obey Christ," wrote Paul (2 Corinthians 10:5, *TEV*). The message of Philippians 4:7,8 should be taken seriously.

Sexual Intercourse

Sexual intercourse (also called coitus or copulation) is the physical union of a man and woman in which the man's erect penis is placed inside the woman's vagina. The in-and-out movement of the penis then produces pleasurable sensations in both partners, and the act of intercourse climaxes in an automatic nerve-reflex action involving a series of muscular spasms called *orgasm*. At this time, semen is ejaculated from the penis into the vagina. The Bible makes clear that sexual intercourse is to take place only between a husband and wife.

In a sense, sexual intercourse is like a three-act drama. First, there is usually a period of *foreplay* or petting between the partners. Then the intromission of the penis into the vagina, culminating in the ejaculation of semen. Afterwards, there is usually a period of *afterglow* in which the husband and wife continue to lie close together while the penis is still erect. This is a time of feeling content, loving and warm toward one another, with a deep sense of satisfaction and relaxation. Words of endearment, kisses, and tender caresses may continue at this time.

A husband and wife don't always experience their orgasms at the same moment. Sometimes they do, at other times, the husband might reach a climax before his wife. Where this is true he should help her to reach her orgasm by stroking her "mons area" with his hand. At still other times, a wife may reach a sexual climax before her husband, perhaps during foreplay. Perhaps she'll have additional orgasms during the actual union as well. Sometimes she may have a very mild orgasm or even none at all, and yet find the sex experience with her husband enjoyable and meaningful. Then, they may find that at other times, she may experience such an intense, explosive orgasm that it seems like the Fourth of July when all the fireworks go off at one time! This is emphasized because recognition of a woman's sexual potential is fairly recent, and many husbands and wives are not yet aware of how pleasurable and meaningful this can make the act of love for both of them. On the other hand, couples should not become victimized by what someone has called "the tyranny of the orgasm." They should not take too seriously the insistence in some marriage manuals that a couple *must* strive toward having simultaneous, mutual orgasms, with the implication being that the sex act is a failure otherwise. This can make sex seem like work rather than enjoyment, and much of the joy of spontaneity and individualized innovativeness is lost because of mistaken ideas about "the right way." Couples should learn to relax and enjoy one another and express their love in whatever way pleases them both. They'll find there's always more to learn, for the delights of love can grow over the years as their affection for one another grows and their marriage relationship deepens.

Difficulties with regard to sexual response in marriage may take the form of impotence (in the male) or frigidity (in the female). *Impotence* means that a man is unable to achieve or maintain an erection of the penis, with the result that intercourse is impossible. *Frigidity* usually refers to the inability of a woman to experience sexual pleasure. Instead of warmth, excitement and responsiveness in sex relations, there may be indifference, a sense of distaste, revulsion, and coldness (hence the name, frigid). Sometimes the term is reserved for the inability to achieve orgasm, but the broader definition seems more accurate and is being increasingly used. Impotence and frigidity usually have psychological causes, but occasionally there may be physiological causes for the difficulty.

Discussing Sexual
Intercourse with Your Children
Many parents are able to answer the earliest questions

about reproduction without embarrassment. It isn't too hard to say that a baby grows inside a special place God made in a mother's body, or that the baby began as a wee, tiny egg that was joined by a special sperm cell, or even that the sperm cell came from the daddy's body. But it's the anticipation of the big question—"How does the daddy put the sperm cell in the mommy?"—that makes parents nervous, flustered and tongue-tied.

Such fears and nervousness should not be necessary. If a child is old enough to ask about sex, he's old enough to be told the truth. Simply explain that God has designed the father's body so that sperm cells are made in a little bag of skin that hangs between his legs. God has also designed the father's penis so that it will fit into a special opening in the mother's body—the vagina. Because a husband and wife love each other, they want to be as close together as possible. God designed their bodies to fit together just perfectly. At special times as they lie together in bed, a husband and wife show their love for each other by joining together. The father places his penis into the mother's vagina. Sperm cells pass through his penis into the vagina, and then swim up into the uterus and tubes, where they may meet a tiny egg cell. If a sperm joins with an egg, a baby begins to grow inside the wife. When a husband and wife show their love in this special way, it's called "sexual intercourse," or "sex relations."

God's design of male and female bodies to fit together this way is really very marvelous and nothing to be ashamed of. One mother missed an opportunity to explain sexual intercourse to her daughter because the question came up in an unusual way and the mother wasn't prepared to handle it. They were shopping at a hardware store to pick up a male and female hose coupling. The girl began to giggle. "How can anybody call parts for a garden hose 'boys' and 'girls'?" she laughed.

"Daddy must be playing a joke on us!" The mother flushed and said, "No, that's the real name for those parts. The one with the opening is called the female, and the one that fits into it is called the male coupling." "But *why* Mom?" asked the girl, to which her mother replied, "It's just the custom." She was too embarrassed to explain the correspondence to the human body.

Of course, sexual intercourse is more than "fitting together." And it's also more than procreation. Some children have the impression that husbands and wives have sex relations only in connection with having a baby. Thus a child may tell a friend, "My parents did it three times. Yours must have done it twice because you only have one sister." The procreative side of sex is important and more easily understood by children. But school-age children can also begin understanding that there is an emotional-pleasurable-communicative side to sexual intercourse.

At the appropriate time you can explain that husbands and wives like to show their love in this special way. Perhaps you can say, "You know how you like that happy, warm feeling of being cuddled and told we love you? Look how many times you say, 'Hug me Mommy!' or 'Squeeze me real tight, Daddy.' Well, it's something like that with a husband and wife. They love each other very, very much. They like to hug and kiss and be very close to each other. God made their bodies in a special way so that they can be so close it's like being one person—because that's what God says being married is supposed to be like. Although married couples show their love in lots of other ways, God planned sexual intercourse as a very *special* way of showing their oneness."

Teen-agers may wonder about specific details. They might have questions about frequency. Research indicates that twice a week is the average for married couples, though some might have sex relations much more often than that and others less often. Or they might wonder about how long sexual intercourse takes. The duration varies just as the frequency does. Some couples spend only ten minutes or less in their lovemaking, while others may spend a half hour, forty-five minutes or longer, giving considerable time to foreplay. The duration may vary not only between couples but in the case of a particular couple from time to time. Teens also might be curious about positions. It can be explained that there is no *one* way of embracing sexually, no "right" position. Husbands and wives may lie side by side or with either one above and the other underneath, as well as a variety of other ways.

Sterility and Sterilization

Sterility or infertility simply means that a man or a woman is physically incapable of becoming a parent of a child. Difficulties in the reproduction system, whether resulting from glandular disturbances, malfunctioning of reproductive organs, disease or any other cause, make it impossible for a sterile person to perform the male or female role in producing offspring.

Sterility may result from natural causes or it may be brought about through various types of surgical procedures. In the latter case, the term *sterilization* is used and refers to the act of making an individual incapable of producing offspring. Sometimes an operation which results in the sterilization of an individual is performed because of a diseased state involving the reproductive organs, as in the case of cancer of the uterus. In other cases, a person may elect to have an operation as a means of permanent birth control. This is called *voluntary sterilization*.

A simple fifteen-minute operation to accomplish sterilization in males may be performed in a physician's office under a local anesthetic. Called a *vasectomy,* the operation is growing in popularity among married men who no longer desire to have children. The surgical procedure involves the cutting of the tubes (vas deferens) which carry the sperm cells from the testicles to the urethra. In some cases the process is reversible and fertility can be restored through a later surgical procedure. But this is not always true and should not be counted on when making the decision about whether or not a vasectomy is desirable. Men who have a vasectomy do not lose their sex drive, maleness, or ability to have sexual intercourse, including the ability to ejaculate seminal fluid. The only difference is that the semen will not contain sperm cells. The testicles will continue to produce sperm, but the vasectomy results in a "roadblock" that stops them from passing from the body. The sperm cells are simply reabsorbed into the body and cause no swelling or other problem.

Vasectomy should *not* be confused with castration, an operation in which the testicles are removed. Castration before puberty prevents a boy's development of secondary sex characteristics such as a beard and a lowered voice, as well as making him incapable of fatherhood. Castrated males during Bible times were called eunuchs (cf. Isaiah 56:3-5; Deuteronomy 23:1; Matthew 19:12; Acts 8:27). In the ancient world eunuchs were often employed as harem guards and palace officials.

In female sterilization, the most common operation is the cutting and tying of the Fallopian tubes sometimes called "tubal ligation." After such surgery, the ovum released each month cannot be reached by sperm cells, which are now blocked from entering the tubes. The ovum is simply absorbed.

Sterilization also occurs if both ovaries are removed (because ovum production ceases) or if the uterus is removed (hysterectomy).

This Subject and Your Child

Questions about sterility may arise as children wonder why some people can't have babies. They can be answered simply and told that the bodies of some people don't function in the way necessary to reproduce. Some men can't produce enough sperm, and some women can't produce mature eggs or aren't able to nourish a developing baby in the uterus.

Questions about sterilization sometimes come up in connection with having a pet spayed. In spaying, the ovaries of a female cat or dog are removed. Children may wonder if humans ever have operations that make it impossible for them to have babies. The answer is yes. Some people do have operations that will not let them have more babies than they can love and care for.

Teen-agers, aware of the population pressures in today's world, may wish to know more details about sterilization, including ethical considerations for Christians. The Christian Medical Society's report on the 1968 Protestant Symposium on the Control of Human Reproduction[60] deals with these aspects of sterilization in a helpful way.

Venereal Diseases

Venereal diseases, sometimes called "social diseases" because of the way they are spread, are serious diseases contracted through sexual relations. They are spread from person to person in direct *sexual* contact and are *not* caught from contaminated towels, doorknobs, sheets or toilet seats.[61]

It should be understood that the contracting of VD always involves more than two persons. That is, a man and woman who have never had sexual contact with anyone else aren't going to develop VD simply through having sexual intercourse together on their wedding night. Intercourse in itself doesn't cause venereal disease. Rather, there must be intercourse *with an infected person* if the disease is to develop. If a person contracts a venereal disease, it means that his or her sexual partner has had sex relations with somebody—who already has the disease. This is sometimes a hard fact to accept, especially when a wife finds she has VD and it comes to light that her husband has been having an extramarital affair.

The two most common venereal diseases in our country are *gonorrhea* and *syphilis*. Both are caused by specific germs. Both are spread through sexual intercourse. In addition, syphilis may also be contracted through kissing an infected person. Both can be cured through penicillin if treated in the early stages, but both can cause extremely serious consequences if left untreated. Any persons suspecting that they may have a venereal disease should see a doctor immediately.

Untreated syphilis can cause blindness, deafness, insanity, heart disease, paralysis, and even death. Untreated gonorrhea may result in sterility, heart damage and arthritis. An untreated mother infected with syphilis may give birth to a baby which is mentally retarded, blind or deaf. To prevent blindness in babies whose mothers might have gonorrhea, all states have laws requiring the routine use of silver nitrate drops in infants' eyes immediately after birth.

The first sign of syphilis is usually a sore, called a chancre, that appears where the germs entered the body, usually on the sex organs, although it might also appear on the mouth or elsewhere. It appears several weeks after sexual contact and lasts for about a month. After the appearance of the chancre, other signs might show up, such as a rash, sore throat, fever, headaches, and loss of hair. Eventually the signs disappear, but if untreated, the germ remains in the body and can cause extremely serious trouble later on. In addition, the person may spread the disease to other persons.

Gonorrhea, more common than syphilis, has different symptoms. In males, a few days after contracting the disease from an infected person, painful, burning urination is noticed. In addition, there is a pus-like discharge. In females, the signs of gonorrhea are not so easily noticed because they are usually less acute, although there may be swelling of the Bartholin's glands, an unusual vaginal discharge, and redness and tenderness around the vagina. (Syphilis is also more apt to go undetected in women, because the sore may be hidden from view, in the vagina or cervix.)

Anyone who suspects VD should see a physician without delay.

This Subject and Your Child

Children approaching adolescence should be aware of the dangers of VD, how it is spread, and should have some knowledge of the signs that show up in connection with both syphilis and gonorrhea. A helpful, simple pamphlet suitable for reading by junior-high and high-school young people is called, "Some Questions and Answers about VD." It's available for 5¢ from the American Social Health Association, 1740 Broadway, New York, NY. 10019.

References

1. Lawrence Q. Crawley, James L. Malfetti, Ernest I. Stewart, and Nina Vas Dias, *Reproduction, Sex, and Preparation for Marriage* (Englewood Cliffs, N.J.: Prentice-Hall, Inc., 1964. Also Jane E. Broday, "Abortion: The Medical and Psychological View," *Woman's Day* (October, 1970), pp. 68 ff.

2. Walter O. Spitzer and Carlyle L. Saylor, eds., *Birth Control and the Christian* (Wheaton, Ill.: Tyndale House Publishers, 1969). Also R. F. R. Gardner, *Abortion: The Personal Dilemma* (Grand Rapids, Mich.: Wm. B. Eerdmans Pub. Co., 1972).

3. Valentina Wasson, *The Chosen Baby* (Philadelphia: J. B. Lippincott Co., 1951).

4. Eda LeShan, *You and Your Adopted Child* (New York: Public Affairs Pamphlet, No. 274, 1958), pp. 10-12.

5. Ibid., p. 5.

6. Ibid, p. 20.

7. Dr. V. Elving Anderson, as quoted in James C. Hefley, *Adventures with God* (Grand Rapids: Zondervan Pub. House, 1967), p. 110.

8. See footnote 2 above.

9. Alfred M. Rehwinkel, *Planned Parenthood* (St. Louis: Concordia Pub. House, 1959).

10. Lloyd Saxton, *The Individual, Marriage, and the Family* (Belmont, Cal.: Wadsworth Pub. Co., 1968), p. 81.

11. David Reuben, M.D., *Everything You Always Wanted to Know About Sex* (New York: Bantam paperback edition, 1969), pp. 83-84. Also see John Oliven, M.D., "Answers to Questions," *Sexual Behavior*, Vol. 1, No. 3 (Aug., 1971), p. 13.

12. James L. Mathis, M.D., "The Exhibitionist," *Medical Aspects of Human Sexuality*, Vol. III, No. 6 (June, 1969), p. 92.

13. Ibid., p. 93.

14. E. M. Blaiklock, in a letter to the author, January 17, 1968. Used by permission.

15. See Letha Scanzoni, *Sex and the Single Eye* (Grand Rapids: Zondervan, 1968), pp. 114-123.

16. Paul H. Gebhard, "Incidence of Overt Homosexuality in the United States and Western Europe," in John M. Livingood, ed., *National Institute of Mental Health Task Force on Homosexuality: Final Report and Background Papers* (DHEW Publication No. [HSM] 72-9116, printed 1972), p. 26. The entirety of this report is available for 75¢ from the Superintendent of Documents, U.S. Gov-

ernment Printing Office, Washington, D.C. 20402 (stock number 1724-0244).

17. For up-to-date information on hormonal factors that may be related to certain cases of homosexuality, see John Money, "Sexual Dimorphism and Homosexual Gender Identity" (pp. 42-54) and his 1972 appendix, "Pubertal Hormones and Homosexuality, Bisexuality and Heterosexuality" (pp. 73-77) in the *National Institute of Mental Health Task Force on Homosexuality: Final Report and Background Papers.*

18. Robert R. Bell, *Social Deviance* (Homewood, Ill.: The Dorsey Press, 1971), p. 263. Also Norman Pittenger, "The Homosexual Expression of Love," in *Is Gay Good?— Ethics, Theology, and Homosexuality*, ed. by W. Dwight Oberholtzer (Philadelphia: The Westminster Press, 1971), pp. 228,229.

19. Oscar E. Feucht, ed., *Sex and the Church* (St. Louis: Concordia Publ. House, 1961), p. 24.

20. Bell, *Social Deviance*, p. 249.

21. C.B. Scrignar, M.D., "Sex and the Under-Aged Girl," *Medical Aspects of Human Sexuality*, Vol. II, No. 12 (Dec., 1968), p. 39.

22. C.S. Lewis, *The Four Loves* (London: Fontana Books paperback edition, 1963), pp. 57-58.

23. Wardell B. Pomeroy, Ph.D., "Parents and Homosexuality," in *Sex in the Adolescent Years*, edited by Isadore Rubin, Ph.D., and Lester A. Kirkendall, Ph.D. (New York: Association Press, 1968), p. 175. Also see Pomeroy, *Boys and Sex* (New York: Dell Paperback edition, 1968), pp. 59-60,151.

24. Pomeroy (in Rubin and Kirkendall), pp. 177-179.

25. See chapter 7, "What Is Marriage?" in Scanzoni, *Sex and the Single Eye.*

26. The Youth for Christ magazine, *Campus Life* commissioned Phil Landrum to write an article about autoeroticism based on interviews with authors of cur-

rent Christian books on sex. The staff was surprised to find amazingly similar views on masturbation expressed by all five authors: Charlie Shedd, author of *The Stork Is Dead* (Word): Jim Hefley, author of *Sex, Sense & Nonsense* (David C. Cook); Letha Scanzoni, author of *Sex and the Single Eye* (Zondervan); M. O. Vincent, M.D., author of *God, Sex and You* (Lippincott), and Herbert J. Miles, Ph.D., author of *Sexual Understanding Before Marriage* (Zondervan). See "But What About Right Now?" *Campus Life* (March, 1972), pp. 38-42.

27. Saxton, *The Individual, Marriage and the Family*, p. 142.

28. T. W. Shannon, *Eugenics or the Laws of Sex Life and Heredity* (Marietta, Ohio: The S.A. Mullikin Co., 1917), pp. 262-263. This book was recently reissued by Doubleday in a replica edition.

29. Saxton, *The Individual, Marriage and the Family*, pp. 142-43.

30. See Pomeroy, *Boys and Sex*, p. 42. Also see Sex Information and Education Council of the United States, *Sexuality and Man* (New York: Charles Scribner's Sons, 1970), pp. 66-67.

31. See Frank A. Lawes, *The Sanctity of Sex* (Chicago; Good News Publishers, 1948); and W. Melville Capper and H. Morgan Williams, *Heirs Together* (Chicago: Inter-Varsity Christian Fellowship, 1948). A more recent book speaks of masturbation in terms of self-indulgence and a lack of control over one's passions. Hence, "such self-gratification carries with it the wish to rebel against God's authority over our bodies." See C. G. Scorer, *The Bible and Sex Ethics Today* (Downers Grove, Ill.: Inter-Varsity Press, 1966), p. 84. David Wilkerson has said, "Masturbation is not a gift of God for release of sex drives. Masturbation is not normal behavior and is not condoned in the Scriptures." See *Jesus Person Maturity*

Manual (Glendale, California: Regal Books Division, G/L Publications, 1971), p. 53.

32. See Walter Trobisch, *My Parents Are Impossible* (Downers Grove, Ill.: Inter-Varsity Press); Clyde M. Narramore, *Life and Love* (Grand Rapids: Zondervan, 1956); and Thomas O. Howard, *An Antique Drum* (Philadelphia: J.B. Lippincott Co., 1969). A variation of this view is found in Bruce Larson's *Ask Me to Dance* (Waco, Texas: Word Books, 1972), where he writes that, for both single and married persons, masturbation is "not God's best" because it is a way of taking one's destiny in one's own hands and trying to provide for one's own sexual needs rather than trusting God (p. 100). A similar stance is taken by Gladys Hunt in her chapter on singleness in *Ms. Means Myself* (Grand Rapids: Zondervan, 1972).

33. This present author would place herself in this "Christian liberty" category, as would James Hefley (see article cited in footnote 26).

34. Herbert J. Miles, *Sexual Understanding Before Marriage* (Grand Rapids: Zondervan, 1971), pp. 137-177. A similar view seems to come through in William Fitch, *Christian Perspectives on Sex and Marriage* (Wm. B. Eerdmans Pub. Co., 1971), p. 123.

35. William H. Masters and Virginia E. Johnson, "Female Sexuality," in Martha Stuart and William T. Liu, eds., *The Emerging Woman* (Boston: Little, Brown, and Co., 1970), pp. 101-102.

36. M. O. Vincent, M.D., *God, Sex and You* (Philadelphia: J.B. Lippincott Co., 1971), pp. 142-144.

37. *Ibid.*, p. 144.

38. Charlie W. Shedd, *The Stork Is Dead* (Waco, Texas: Word Books, 1968), p. 73.

39. Richard S. Hettlinger, *Living With Sex: The Student's Dilemma* (New York: Seabury Press, 1966).

40. Phil Landrum, "But What About Right Now?" *Campus Life* (March, 1972), p. 41.

41. Sex Information and Education Council of the United States, *Sexuality and Man* (New York: Charles Scribner's Sons, 1970), p. 69.

42. Lester A. Kirkendall, "Understanding the Male Sex Drive," in Rubin and Kirkendall, eds., *Sex in the Adolescent Years* (New York: Association Press, 1968), p. 50.

43. Ibid., p. 51.

44. Ibid., p. 52.

45. Ibid., p. 52.

46. *Sexuality and Man,* p. 63; also see Pomeroy, *Boys and Sex,* p. 40.

47. Crawley, *et al., Reproduction, Sex and Preparation for Marriage,* p. 26. Also see Mary Steichen Calderone, *Release from Sexual Tensions* (New York: Random House, 1960), pp. 192-193.

48. Calderone, *Release from Sexual Tensions,* pp. 200-202.

49. See the chapter entitled, "The Abominations of Leviticus," in Mary Douglas, *Purity and Danger* (Middlesex, England: Penguin Books, Ltd., Pelican Books edition, 1970), pp. 54-72.

50. Fred E. D'Amour, *Basic Physiology* (Chicago: University of Chicago Press, 1961), pp. 477-478.

51. M.O. Vincent, *God, Sex and You,* p. 22.

52. Elisabeth Elliot, *The Liberty of Obedience* (Waco, Texas: Word Books, Publishers, 1968), pp. 16-17.

53. Lester A. Kirkendall, "Understanding the Problems of the Male Virgin," in Rubin and Kirkendall, eds., *Sex in the Adolescent Years,* pp. 123-129.

54. From *The Report of the Commission on Obscenity and Pornography,* September, 1970, as reprinted in Robert R. Bell and Michael Gordon, eds., *The Social Dimension of Human Sexuality* (Boston: Little, Brown and Co., 1972), p. 288.

55. Bell and Gordon, "Commercialized Sex," *The Social Dimension of Human Sexuality,* p. 229.

56. Lester A. Kirkendall and David S. Brody, "The Arousal of Fear—Does It Have a Place in Sex Education," *The Family Life Coordinator,* Vol. XIII, No. 1 (Jan., 1964), pp. 14-16.

57. C. B. Scrignar, M.D., "Sex and the Under-Aged Girl," *Medical Aspects of Human Sexuality,* Vol. II, No. 12 (Dec., 1968), p. 39.

58. *Saint Jerome, Epistle xxii* (to Eustochium).

59. Philip R. Sullivan, M.D., "What Is the Role of Fantasy in Sex?" *Medical Aspects of Human Sexuality,* Vol. III, No. 4 (April, 1969), p. 82.

60. Walter O. Spitzer and Carlyle L. Saylor, eds., *Birth Control and the Christian* (Wheaton, Ill.: Tyndale House Publishers, 1969).

61. See the American Social Health Association's pamphlet, "Some Questions and Answers about VD." Also see Elaine C. Pierson, *Sex Is Never an Emergency* (A Candid Guide for College Students) (Philadelphia: J. B. Lippincott Co., 1971), p. 30.

CHAPTER NINE

Books to Aid Parents in Their Task as Sex Educators

General Books and Series

The Concordia Sex Education Series, W. J. Fields, editor. A graded program of Christian sex education for use in homes and churches. Both books and filmstrips are available. Parents will be interested in the following colorful, well-written books which integrate biological facts with reverent Christian attitudes toward human sexuality:

I Wonder, I Wonder by Marguerite Kurth Frey, M.D. A story book for children aged 5-8. It tells of two small children who learn about the wonder of reproduction when twins are born into the family.

Wonderfully Made by Ruth Hummel. Children aged 9-11 learn the facts of life through this book they can read for themselves.

Take the High Road, by A.J. Beultmann. A book for 12- to 14-year-olds.

Life Can Be Sexual by Elmer N. Witt. A book for adolescents 15 years of age and older, which tries to help young people sort through attitudes, conduct and sex ethics in a well-reasoned manner. Biblical but not "preachy." Two other books in the series are especially

247

helpful for adults: *Christian View of Sex Education* by Martin F. Wessler, and *Parents' Guide to Christian Conversation About Sex* by Erwin J. Kolb. Published by Concordia Publishing House, 3558 South Jefferson Ave., St. Louis, Mo. 63118.

AMA Sex Education Series, a series of inexpensive pamphlets published by The Joint Committee of Health Problems in Education of the National Education Association and the American Medical Association.

Parents' Responsibility, for parents of young children.

A Story About You, for children in grades 4-6.

Finding Yourself, for junior-high young people.

Approaching Adulthood, for older teen-agers. Published by the American Medical Association, 535 N. Dearborn, Chicago, Ill. 60610.

Kimberly-Clark Life Cycle Library, a series of six inexpensive pamphlets for girls and young women from puberty through engagement, marriage and first pregnancy. Well-illustrated. Order from The Life Cycle Center, Kimberly-Clark Corp., Neenah, Wis. 54956.

The Life Cycle Library. Not to be confused with the above series, this set of four hardback books and a paperback "answer book" for parents is published by the Parent and Child Institute, Chicago. Three volumes explain the basic facts of sex and reproduction, and a fourth consists of a thorough glossary of sex terms. Particularly suitable for homes with children of junior high age. Available from Weekly Reader Family Book Service, American Education Publications, Education Center, Columbus, Ohio 43216.

What to Tell Your Children About Sex. Answers to questions children of different ages ask about sex. Child Study Association of America, 9 East 89th Street, New York, New York 10028.

A Guide for Christian Sex Education of Youth by Thomas Edwards Brown (New York: Association Press,

1968). Designed primarily as a guide for churches and communities interested in providing sex education programs for junior-high and high-school young people, this book will also be informative for parents. It describes the questions and conflicts adolescents have about sex and gives examples of wise answers and counsel.

Books for Younger Children

A *Baby Is Born* by Milton I. Levine, M.D., and Jean H. Seligmann (New York: Golden Press, 1949). Now in its twenty-first printing, this book emphasizes the wonder of life and warm family love as it explains how a child enters the world from the tiniest of beginnings. Pictures are specific but tasteful. Animal reproduction is discussed as well as human reproduction, but the unique difference in human sexuality is emphasized.

The Beginning of Life by Eva Knox Evans. (New York: Macmillan, 1969). Conception, pregnancy and childbirth are simply and clearly explained. Could be read aloud to younger children or read directly by the child beginning at about age eight.

Growing Up by Karl de Schweinitz (New York: MacMillan, 1963 edition). The story of how both people and animals "become alive, are born, and grow."

The Story of You by Edgar and Ada Milam Cockefair (Monona Publications, P.O. Box 3222, Madison, Wis. 53704, 1955). Simple explanation of the ongoingness of human life, written for preschoolers.

Susie's Babies by E. Margaret Clarkson (Grand Rapids, Mich.: Wm. B. Eerdmans Publishing Co., 1960). An excellent introduction to the facts of life, with Christian teaching woven into a fascinating story about a hamster and her babies and the lessons children learn from observing her.

The Wonderful Story of How You Were Born by Sidonie

Matsner Gruenberg (Garden City, N.Y.: Doubleday & Co., Inc., 1970 edition). One of the most beautiful books written on the subject. Well-written with warmth, joy and sensitivity in both the pictures and the text, this book explains sex to children in a way that elicits wonder and appreciation of life, love, marriage and family living. The description of sexual intercourse is outstanding in the way it combines honesty with an attitude of tenderness and reverence.

Books for Children in Grades Six Through Eight

Chats with Young People on Growing Up by E. Margaret Clarkson (Grand Rapids: Wm. B. Eerdmans Pub. Co., 1962). This sequel to *Susie's Babies* again uses the observation of a hamster, this time to teach lessons of emotional and sexual maturity.

Facts about Sex by Sol Gordon (New York: The John Day Co., 1970). A short, direct, and frank book about sex "for young people who really do not like to read but who *want to know*," written on the sixth-grade reading level. Very vivid but tasteful drawings illustrate sex differences, pregnancy, and birth.

Love and Sex in Plain Language by Eric W. Johnson (Philadelphia: J. B. Lippincott Co., 1965). An excellent clear explanation of the basic facts about sex in language junior-high-age young people will understand. Also available in a Bantam Pathfinder paperback edition.

Sex—Telling It Straight by Eric W. Johnson (Philadelphia: J. B. Lippincott Co., 1970). Similar to the above book in material covered, this book is especially designed for youngsters growing up "where hardship is one of the facts of life," in urban ghettos or in rural areas—any situation in which children may be exposed to sex early in life "through observation, conversation, and experience," and who thus need accurate information and guidance.

Books for Teen-agers and College-Age Young People

The Bible and Sex Ethics Today by C. G. Scorer (Downers Grove, Ill.: Inter-Varsity Press, 1966). In this helpful examination of Biblical teachings on sex, a British surgeon provides guidance for youth seeking to work out sexual standards consistent with faith in Christ. (Paperback.)

Christian Perspectives on Sex and Marriage by William Fitch (Grand Rapids, Mich.: William B. Eerdmans Publishing Co., 1971). The author is a Canadian minister with many years experience in counseling husbands and wives and engaged couples. This book is largely a summary of his Scripture-based marriage counseling. It provides both factual information and ethical guidance. (Paperback.)

God, Sex and You—An Evangelical Perspective (Philadelphia: J. B. Lippincott Co., 1971). The author, M. O. Vincent, is a noted psychiatrist, as well as being a committed Christian. He understands young people and their questions about sex, and he understands what the Bible says about sex. Both aspects of his understanding come through well in this very fine book.

I Loved a Girl (including *I Loved a Young Man*) by Walter Trobisch (New York: Harper & Row Chapelbook edition, 1965). A missionary-pastor shares his frank correspondence with a young African man and woman about love, courtship, sex, and marriage.

I Married You by Walter Trobisch (New York: Harper & Row, 1971). A story and discussion of God's plan for marriage. Easy, enjoyable reading with a message.

The Other Side of Morality by Fritz Ridenour (Glendale, Calif.: Regal Books, 1969). For young people (and their parents) who are confused about "situation ethics," "the new morality," and "the Playboy philosophy," this book provides biblically-based answers.

Love, Sex and Being Human by Paul Bohannan (Garden City, N.Y.: Doubleday & Co., Inc. paperback edition, 1970). Both the biological and emotional side of human sexuality are clearly presented with teen-agers in mind.

Reproduction, Sex and Preparation for Marriage by Lawrence Q. Crawley, James L. Malfetti, Ernest I. Stewart, and Nina Vas Dias (Englewood Cliffs, N.J.: Prentice-Hall, Inc., 1964). Written especially with college students in mind, this book contains a clear and factual discussion of sex, answering the many questions young adults have about this important aspect of life. Available in paperback.

The Returns of Love—A Contemporary Christian View of Homosexuality by Alex Davidson (Inter-Varsity Press, 1970). This book calls for Christian understanding and compassion toward those who struggle with homosexual temptations. It consists of letters written by a Christian young man undergoing such struggles and trying to deal with them in the light of his faith in Christ. Distinguishes between homosexual acts and a homosexual "condition."

Sex and the Single Eye by Letha Scanzoni (Grand Rapids: Zondervan Publishing House, 1968). A Christian philosophy of sex addressing itself especially to the questions and concerns of Christian young adults in colleges and universities today. Suitable for older high school students also.

Sexual Happiness in Marriage by Herbert J. Miles (Grand Rapids: Zondervan Publishing House, 1967). A high view of the Bible and a high view of sex in marriage are combined in this helpful book, providing guidance for engaged and married couples. Techniques for sexual enjoyment in marriage are included.

The Stork Is Dead by Charlie W. Shedd (Waco, Texas: Word Books, 1968). An extremely frank and forthright book, answering (in language teens appreciate) the questions modern youth are asking about dating, petting, sex, and marriage.

Why Wait Till Marriage? by Evelyn Millis Duvall (New York: Association Press, 1965). Although not directly addressed to Christian young people whose sex standards should be based on commitment to Christ rather than on fears of the consequences of premarital experimentation, the book does contain some good commonsense reasons for chastity and helpful advice for young men and women.

Young People and Sex by Dr. Arthur H. Cain (New York: John Day Co., 1967). This book presents high moral standards, a clear description of the biological facts of sex, guidance for sexual behavior, and some wise suggestions for steering clear of sexual temptations in dating situations.

For Serious Study

Birth Control and the Christian, edited by Walter O. Spitzer and Carlyle L. Saylor (Wheaton, Ill.: Tyndale House Publishers, 1969). Christians in the fields of medicine, theology, psychology, sociology and law provide guidance and understanding with regard to such subjects as contraception, abortion and sterilization.

Sex and the Church, edited by Oscar E. Feucht (St. Louis: Concordia Pub. House, 1961). An overview of biblical and church teachings on the subject of sex over the ages.

A list of this sort must necessarily be brief, with the result that many fine books which parents and children may find helpful are not included. But it is hoped that at least the list will get parents started on a quest for worthwhile materials to include in a program of sex education in the home. Take time to browse in libraries and bookstores and to look through catalogues of various publishers.

When you do find suitable books for your children, take time to read the books yourself and be prepared to discuss them with your children. If a book provides the physical facts but lacks a Christian emphasis, you can provide that emphasis as you discuss the book's content together. As a parent committed to Jesus Christ, you are not only asked to be a *sex* educator, you are asked to be a *Christian* sex educator.

Subject Index